Masks from West and Central Africa
A Celebration of Color & Form

Mary Sue Rosen

Paul Peter Rosen

4880 Lower Valley Road • Atglen, PA 19310

Copyright © 2013
by Mary Sue Rosen and Paul Peter Rosen

Library of Congress Control Number: 2013949072

All rights reserved. No part of this work may be reproduced or used in any form or by any means—graphic, electronic, or mechanical, including photocopying or information storage and retrieval systems—without written permission from the publisher.

The scanning, uploading and distribution of this book or any part thereof via the Internet or via any other means without the permission of the publisher is illegal and punishable by law. Please purchase only authorized editions and do not participate in or encourage the electronic piracy of copyrighted materials.

"Schiffer," "Schiffer Publishing, Ltd. & Design," and the "Design of pen and inkwell" are registered trademarks of Schiffer Publishing, Ltd.

Cover Designed by Bruce Waters
Designed by Matthew Goodman
Type set in Visage and Niagara Solid

ISBN: 978-0-7643-4336-0
Printed in Hong Kong

Published by Schiffer Publishing, Ltd.
4880 Lower Valley Road
Atglen, PA 19310
Phone: (610) 593-1777; Fax: (610) 593-2002
E-mail: Info@schifferbooks.com

For the largest selection of fine reference books on this and related subjects, please visit our website at **www.schifferbooks.com**.

You may also write for a free catalog.

This book may be purchased from the publisher.
Please try your bookstore first.

We are always looking for people to write books on new and related subjects. If you have an idea for a book, please contact us at proposals@schifferbooks.com.

Schiffer Books are available at special discounts for bulk purchases for sales promotions or premiums. Special editions, including personalized covers, corporate imprints, and excerpts can be created in large quantities for special needs. For more information contact the publisher.

Contents

Acknowledgment 4
Preface 5

    Masks in this Book 5
    The Styles of African Masks 5
    African Masks as Material Culture 6
    Art, Material Culture, and Tradition in African Masks 7
    Age of African Masks 8
    Copies, Authenticity, and Collecting African Masks 8

Introduction 10

    Background 10
    The Making of African Masks 11
    African Mask Performances (Masquerades) 11

Masks from West and Central Africa 13
References 189
Index of Masks 192

Acknowledgment

In 2011, we were invited to mount an exhibition of African masks at the Free Library in Philadelphia. The exhibition was titled *More Than A Pretty Face: Masks from West and Central Africa*. We extend our most sincere thanks to Siobhan Reardon, President and Chief Executive Officer of the Free Library, for her ongoing support of African art exhibitions that we have had the privilege to offer from our collection. We wish to acknowledge and thank Lynn Washington, Design Studio Supervisor, for her superb assistance with the installation. This book is an outgrowth of the Free Library exhibition. We are indebted to Nancy Schiffer who had the vision to set this writing project in motion, and for allowing it to encompass a much wider representation of masks from West and Central Africa than appeared in the Philadelphia exhibition.

We especially wish to thank John Nunley, the foremost expert on Temne masking practices, for his invaluable advice and commentary that has been incorporated into the descriptions of Temne masks. Eli Bentor, Professor of Art History at Appalachian State University, graciously provided very helpful information and insightful comments on the Nigerian masks, especially those of the Anang people and their masking traditions, as well as other groups in nearby areas.

On many occasions, we have benefited from the insights of other experts on African art, most particularly Jeremiah Cole, Harmer Johnson, Amyas Naegele, Eric Robertson, and David Stiffler. However, they are not responsible for the choice of masks shown here or for the accompanying information and opinions.

Our numerous African friends who have shared their knowledge of African art and culture gained from their personal experiences are also acknowledged. In particular, we wish to thank Mohamed Berete, Alpha Bility, Kaye Diakete, Hady Diane, Moussa Diane, Ousman Diane, Ali Hamza, Goulgoul Ibegart, Algi Jawara, Dembaba Konte, Ali Saidou, and Johnny Sylla. We value their friendship. When traveling in Africa, we were repeatedly reminded of what we had learned from them.

Patricia Kuharic has provided an essential, artful contribution by her preparation of our photographs for publication. She has been extremely helpful with many details surrounding the process of coordinating the visual images with the text and has been a dedicated and thoughtful collaborator throughout the entire process.

We have been fortunate to have access to a multitude of published references in the Robert Goldwater Library of the Metropolitan Museum of Art in New York City and in our personal library. These sources have helped us for many years with the identification of masks and other artwork in our collection, and have also provided important information about how the masks were used. The descriptions of masks offered in this book are an amalgam of information from many sources. Anticipating that listing numerous references with each mask would be repetitious and greatly lengthen the text, we have chosen to cite pertinent sources selectively in the captions and to provide a single, comprehensive bibliography at the conclusion of the volume.

Finally, and perhaps most importantly, we wish to acknowledge all the unnamed African artists who created the masks illustrated in this book. In many instances, the identity of the sculptor, often a blacksmith, a chief, or other community leader, or a specialist carver, was known to members of the village. Others were itinerant carvers who were sometimes summoned because of their acknowledged skill. The masks carved by these artists were not signed, but it is likely that differences in their work were recognizable to members of the community. Outside of Africa, there is now growing interest in detecting evidence that links African sculptures to individual artists or their ateliers. These investigations have sometimes demonstrated that certain sculptures, including masks, were probably the work of one artist or done under an artist's direction, but they have rarely identified the individual by name outside of the contemporary time frame.

Preface

Masks in This Book

Masks illustrated in this book are part of the authors' collection that also includes substantial holdings of African puppets, statues, textiles, pre-coin currency, furniture, and various personal objects. The selection of material in this volume reflects our interests as well as the vagaries of availability and affordability. This is by no means a comprehensive presentation of all of the known forms of masking to be found in West and Central Africa. Having examined a large number of the published books on African masking, many illustrating fine examples from collections held by various individuals and museums, it is apparent that it would be a prodigious task to reach this yet to be accomplished goal.

In the face of this circumstance, all previous books on this subject have also been selective presentations based on material from one or more private collections, museums, or both. These books either provide a general review of African masking traditions or focus on masking in a particular region or a specific ethnic group. In the context of a broad overview of West and Central Africa, this book emphasizes the masks of certain regions and ethnic groups, particularly the Temne people in Sierra Leone and the Anang (Ibibio) people in Nigeria, whose masking traditions have received relatively little attention in past volumes. The focus on the polychrome masks of these two groups stems from the authors' overall interest in the use of color in African art. Because of this bias, the reader will find that a substantial number of the masks included in this volume are activated through the use of natural pigments, paint, beads, cloth and other colorful decorative material.

The Styles of African Masks

The relationships of the parts of an object including their size, shape, degree of abstraction and embellishment constitute its *style*. Because their masks were intended to be the embodiment of spirits rather than representing specific persons or animals, various African people adopted stylistic idioms to depict the characteristic features of their sculptures that range from relatively naturalistic to highly abstract renderings. Even naturalistic masks that represent, for example, a human face, typically consist of generic, non-individualized components. This is well illustrated by the face masks of the Dan people and Mende *sowei* helmet masks. Semi-abstract carvings such as Bamana *chi wara* head crest masks are schematic creations inspired by nature but with highly exaggerated and simplified elements that result in a symbolic representation of the natural form. Some masks have naturalistic and stylized components and others are simply dramatic creations with little or no apparent reference to natural forms, such as the *bedu* plank mask of the Nfana people.

In some instances, proximity of ethnic groups probably played an important role in fostering common forms, such as the bold, prominent eyes in human faces found predominantly in work from the region that encompasses Nigeria, Benin, and Cameroon. Another regional characteristic is the broad, sometimes protruding, forehead indicative of wisdom and character that dominates certain face masks of the Dan people in Liberia and Ivory Coast and the *sowei* helmet masks of neighboring Sierra Leone. On the other hand, certain features of masks are found almost universally in Africa.

White, often in the form of kaolin pigment that is applied to the surfaces of masks, is a reference to the related themes of age, wisdom, the ancestors, and the spirit world throughout much of West and Central Africa.

The styles of African art are based on traditional forms that express aspects of the observed and imagined world of a particular ethnic group. As observed by Erich Herold in *The Art of Africa: Tribal Masks from the Náprstek Museum, Prague*, "The degree of artistic mastery...(of the sculptor)... rested in the originality of the manner in which he used traditional art forms."

The diffusion of stylistic attributes among neighboring peoples, and sometimes more widely, is also partly attributable to the mobility of itinerant carvers who are known to have worked for a number of ethnic groups. While adhering to basic canons of form and design in the community where they were temporarily located, they were in a position to create adaptations based on styles employed by other communities they had visited. In addition, West and Central Africa have for centuries been the scene of migrations by ethnic groups over short and long distances in response to drought, famine, disease, war, invasion, and the expansion or contraction of kingdoms. Although displaced peoples carried their traditions with them and sought to maintain these traditions in new environments, they are also known to have adopted to varying degrees stylistic elements indigenous to their new neighbors who in turn were influenced by the recent arrivals. Finally, communities in certain areas were and, in some instances, continue to be renowned centers of excellence for carving as exemplified by Ikot Ekpene in Nigeria. Such centers produced masks and other carved objects for many different regional ethnic groups on commission or for market sale and were an ideal locus for stylistic cross-fertilization. Thus, itinerant carvers, migration, and regional carving centers were all forces favoring stylistic adaptations and ultimately the evolution of blended styles.

The concept of geographically restricted ethnic styles, sometimes expressed as "one tribe, one style," arose largely during the period of European colonialism when colonial and district boundaries were drawn with little regard to the distribution and movements of indigenous ethnic groups. Recognizing that many ethnic groups remain divided by the current borders of independent African nations, we have indicated the predominant national identity or identities of people according to the stylistic attributes of their masks.

When possible, we have sought to provide a sense of the range of forms to be found in a particular masking tradition by illustrating more than one example of a type of mask. Within the canon of conventions dictated by tradition and heritage, there has usually been sufficient flexibility to allow for interpretation on the part of different carvers. Over time, this led to the creation of individual works of superior quality and to the acceptance of variations in traditional forms while retaining fundamental stylistic attributes that were understood by the community and considered to be desirable.

African Masks as Material Culture

Masks are a form of *material culture*, a term that refers to objects used for and/or created by human action. The tooth of a leopard is created by nature, but it becomes part of the material culture of a society when incorporated into a necklace where it may signify the social standing of the wearer and have ritual significance. Objects created by crafts people, such as blacksmiths, basket makers, potters, weavers of cloth, and carvers, are part of a community's material culture.

African material culture is no more static than, for example, that of the Orient, Europe, or the Americas; it is always in a process of change in response to different, evolving needs, forces, and resources. Therefore, it is not surprising that the forms of masks created to communicate with the spirit world in various African cultures would change as the subject matter of messages evolves. In response to new problems and challenges, new masks are created to carry messages from newly invented spirits. As discussed below, the age of an African mask or other sculpture does not necessarily correlate with its authenticity.

In recent decades, contemporary African masking has undergone substantial evolution that has largely been unappreciated in academic circles. Failure to recognize these changes reflects the continued focus of historians and anthropologists on genres, aesthetics, and styles that are embodied in masks gathered over the past century in museum and private collections, as well as the continued emphasis on these forms in the African art market, especially by leading auction establishments. As observed by Chika Okeke-Agulu in his Introduction to Phyllis Galembo's book, *Maske*, "...while the art of masks and masking in Africa has been transformed with the appropriation of new materials (especially plastics and synthetic paints and fabrics) and new performance resources, the formal significance of these radical developments was hardly noted in art history circles." In fact, there is increasing emphasis on the use of materials and techniques other than carved wood that have created a great variety of styles derived from traditional forms. This phenomenon was described by Sarah Erdman in her memoir of two years spent as a Peace Corps health care worker in Côte d'Ivoire from 1998 to 2000, where she witnessed a masked figure covered in burlap with "eerie eyeholes…pinched unevenly out of a burlap face" during a nocturnal funeral.

Art, Material Culture, and Tradition in African Masks

The word *art,* as it is understood in Western society, is difficult to define in a simple phrase. Art is created through the conscious application of skill, imagination, experience, observation, workmanship, and ingenuity to produce an arrangement of materials (color, sound, light, words, wood, metal, cloth, etc.) that influences the senses, emotions, and/or the intellect of the creator and/or observer. To the extent that an object of material culture elicits a response from the senses, emotions, and/or the intellect of an observer, it may be considered to be a work of art, despite vast differences in the nature of the response among observers. Since the nature of the response may also change over time, there is a temporal element to what components of material culture are deemed to be art.

Prior to the twentieth century, African masks and sculptures in Western collections were generally confined to ethnographic museums as forms of material culture rather than being considered works of art to be presented in art museums. Today, most installations of African material culture are found in art museums that emphasize the artistry of the work.

Although an African language may not have a word that has the complex meaning we ascribed to art, it will have words that express appreciation of workmanship such as extraordinary, exceptional, decorated, and embellished. In this vocabulary, the idea of art applies to objects deliberately, skillfully made by man that are effective for the purpose for which they were created. This is purpose-driven art, not "art for art's sake." Formal qualities, such as balance or distortion, boldness or moderation, delicacy or crudeness, novelty or conformity to a canon, texture, decoration, and color, are factors that contribute to achieving this goal, depending upon the stylistic standards of a particular ethnic group.

To the extent that they can be generalized, the concept of art and the aesthetic criteria by which Africans judged their creations in pre-colonial and colonial societies received little attention from explorers and colonists who occupied their countries or from Western connoisseurs in the first half of the 20th century. Where such criteria have been noted, the African notion closest to the Western idea of art placed considerable emphasis on goodness and effectiveness. A mask was judged to be pleasing and therefore beautiful if it was successful in achieving a goal such as communicating with spirits, enforcing community standards, ensuring a good harvest and fertility, initiating young people to become responsible members of the community, or protecting a village.

This concept of art and the aesthetics of art from the African perspective persists, as expressed in the following conversation with an African friend (personal communication, July 2011):

> **Q:** How do African people judge the aesthetic qualities of a mask or sculpture?
>
> **A:** Most people in the cities are not concerned about art. Back in the bush they would tell you that a piece is good if it has meaning with the spirits.
>
> **Q:** Do you mean if an object brings good fortune, health, solves problems, etc., that is what determines if a piece is a good piece?
>
> **A:** Yes, that's what counts. Not what a piece looks like but what it can do for a person.

The words *tradition* and *traditional* derive from the Latin word, *traditio* that describes the act of handing over or delivering. In this book tradition and traditional are intended to convey the idea of a custom, attitude, institution, act, belief, or style that is established in a community and passed from generation to generation by practice, word of mouth, or written word. We have not used tradition or traditional to imply a temporal condition such as pre-colonial or to suggest an inflexible, immutable, unchanging custom or style.

Age of African Masks

In regard to African art, Erich Herold noted in *The Art of Africa: Tribal Masks from the náprstek Museum, Prague* that "there seems to be a romantic idea that what is old is precious." The age of African objects is difficult to judge since there are no written records documenting their creation. Consequently, age is usually based on when an object is said to have been acquired, supported in some cases by collecting records. Specific stylistic features can be helpful for estimating the age of an object if there is independent documentation that these features belong to a particular era, but in most cases this is not possible. A mask acquired in 1905 that can be found currently (2011) in a private collection or museum might have been created in 1904. We tend to think of it as being over 100 years old, and this is "chronologically" accurate. But if the mask has been kept in favorable conditions, it has essentially been preserved in the same state as when it was collected and would thus be "functionally" about one year-old with respect to its creation. By the same token, an object collected in 1980 that is known to have existed for 30 years prior to 1980 would be "functionally" 61 years old in 2011, but "chronologically" 31 years old in 2011. This is an important concept to keep in mind when passing judgment on the *authenticity* of African art (commonly meaning made primarily for traditional use as opposed to made primarily for sale) on the basis of age, since in most instances the life span of an object prior to its having been collected is not known and it is difficult to judge. *It is wise to remember that all African art, including masks, was new at the time it was created and first used for ritual purposes.*

Most objects of material culture from Africa in Western private and museum collections from Africa that are considered to be art are said to be from the nineteenth and twentieth centuries, except for a relatively small number of objects obtained by explorers and traders prior to the nineteenth century. This applies particularly to those made of wood since older pieces were invariably destroyed by exposure to the climate and insects. We believe that the masks included in this book date from some time in the twentieth century, but precise ages are not known. The appearance of many masks suggests that they were used in a ritual context, but this could not be determined in all instances. It is possible that some of the masks were created specifically for sale and export in which case they are fine reproductions of the traditional forms.

Copies, Authenticity and Collecting African Masks

The making of copies of masks and statues for sale by African carvers has been documented virtually since the first Europeans arrived on the shores of Africa. In the 19th century and earlier, virtually all of the objects now referred to as African art were thought of as the creations of primitive people or fetishes relegated to private "curio cabinets" and ethnographic museum collections. In this context, the word "curio" denotes a rare, unusual, bizarre, or exotic object. The market for this material was largely limited to ethnographic collections assembled by a small number of individuals and museums. Beginning in the first decade of the 20th century, with the growing appreciation of African sculptural objects as art, the demand for the these objects began to grow, leading to increased acquisition of existing pieces used in traditional rituals and expansion of production primarily intended for sale. Consequently, as previously discussed, age alone is not a reliable criterion by which to determine whether a piece of African sculpture was made principally for traditional use or for sale, since works collected more than a century ago may have been intended primarily for export.

Masks kept in private collections or in museums were originally bought from someone in Africa, received as gifts, or obtained by conquest. Before reaching their current destination, they usually passed through the hands of multiple owners as a result of sale or trade. Regardless of what transpired, the masks are referred to as having been *collected*. Some museums funded expeditions that acquired the objects directly in Africa, usually by purchasing them *in situ,* and in the process usually obtained documentation of where they came from and how they were used. However, much of the material found in museums today was donated by private collectors who purchased the objects in Africa or elsewhere from dealers or at auction, so that by the time they entered the purchaser's collection the objects were several steps removed from their African roots. It has also been established that some masks sold in Africa were copies of revered masks and that masks made for ritual use were sometimes sold after having been used in traditional rites in order to obtain funds with which to commission a new mask. The history of many masks prior to being sold was frequently not documented and the provenance in such cases usually begins with the first individual who acquired it for a collection located outside

Africa. If the piece passed through the hands of a dealer or collector recognized as knowledgeable, it is more likely to be deemed authentic, whereas absence of such provenance or documentary information often leads to an object being labeled as inauthentic or a fake. In this context, the word fake conveys the idea that the object was made solely for sale in a manner intended to create the impression that it had been made for and used in a ritual context. Although a variety of objects can be labeled as fakes according to this definition on the basis of inspection, in some cases it is a judgment influenced by the absence of provenance as well as appearances. The situation is further complicated by the development of considerable skill among African carvers in giving masks and other objects the appearance of age and ritual use that can deceive experts.

Of course, the issue of detecting fakes or forgeries is not limited to tribal art. There have been many instances involving artwork of various genres and time periods. A recent example will serve to highlight the significant points as reported by Patricia Cohen in a December 2011 *New York Times* article under the heading, "FBI Looks Into Possible Forgery of Modern Art." At issue is the authenticity of at least 20 paintings attributed to modern artists such as Jackson Pollack and Mark Rothko sold by reputable American galleries. By way of provenance, the artwork was said to have been obtained by the galleries from a collector living outside the United States who claimed to have inherited them from his father. The father purportedly bought the works directly from the artists. The article noted that "the investigation has riven the art world and underscored how often experts cannot agree on a painting's authenticity."

In this case, the allegations of fraud depended heavily on the limited documented provenance available for most of the paintings. The legend for a picture included in the article referred to it as the image of "...a painting once exhibited as a Jackson Pollack. In 2003, an independent art research group declined to authenticate it for a potential buyer, citing unanswered questions about it's provenance." Referring to the artist Richard Diebenkorn, an expert on his work is quoted as saying, "If I don't have documented provenance of a work, we are immediately very skeptical." Analysis of paint used in two works by Robert Motherwell detected the presence of pigments not "invented until at least 10 years after the date of the paintings."

From the foregoing, several points emerge that apply equally to African art. First, by simply looking at and studying a work, experts can come to different conclusions about its authenticity. Secondly, it is possible to create a "fake" that can deceive many experts, causing them to depend on provenance and in some cases scientific evidence to assess authenticity. Third, provenance can be fabricated, or it may simply document the history of ownership without actually proving who actually created the work (in the case of modern art) or why it was created and whether it was used (in the case of tribal art).

In the final analysis, the collector of African art must be guided first by an appreciation of the artful qualities of one or more genres or styles. The more material a collector is exposed to in museums, galleries, other collections, and publications, the more experience and knowledge an individual will have with which to make additions to a collection. Sometimes, the inherent appeal and aesthetic quality of an object will overrule uncertainty about authenticity or a lack of provenance.

In this book, the text concentrates mainly on ethnographic information that may not be readily available to the reader, while pointing out salient formal features that characterize the mask. It is left to the reader to form an opinion about the aesthetic merits of a particular mask to the degree that this can be achieved from examining the images provided.

As collectors, the authors have been driven by an interest in and appreciation of the artistic qualities of African material culture that has fueled a quest to become more informed about the context in which the objects were created and used. We don't view collecting African art as an either/or enterprise; it is a multidisciplinary activity that encompasses anthropology and aesthetics. This approach has led us to spend time in Mali attending puppet performances to inform our collection of Malian puppets described in our book, *The Colorful Sogo Bò Puppets of Mali,* published by Schiffer Publishing, Ltd. and to observe traditional weaving in Ghana and Togo in relation to our collection of African textiles.

Introduction

Background

Masks and masked performances (masquerades) are found in virtually every cultural group throughout the world. Masks have been used throughout Africa, dating from examples found on Egyptian mummies such as Tutankhamun, where they served to personify the deceased pharaoh. However, the tradition of masked performances is most widespread and strongest in West and Central Africa, the regions from which the material presented here was obtained. The stylistic diversity of these masks is a manifestation of the large number of African cultures that use masks.

With the notable exception of *sowei* masks used by the women's *Sande* Society in Sierra Leone and Liberia, African masks are usually owned, controlled and danced by men. Nonetheless, a substantial number of masks of various forms used by men represent a female spirit, display feminine features, and portray a woman. Three of the many instances of this phenomenon illustrated in this book are different portrayals of the female water spirit, Mami Wata, the Igbo *mmwo* maiden spirit mask in Nigeria, and the *mwanapwo* masks of the Chokwe people in Angola and Democratic Republic of Congo. Women and female ancestors play an important supporting role in men's secret societies such as Poro among the Dan people in Ivory Coast and Liberia whose masquerade rituals embody masculine and feminine spirits.

African masks not only appear on the face or cover the head of the performer, they may also be perched on the forehead, on top of the performer's head, on a shoulder and even on the front or back of the torso. Some masks are carried by the performer, and they may serve as altars. The mask is only part of a costume that envelops most or all of the person (masker) who wears the mask. Although the entire ensemble is essential to bring the mask to life, in the majority of the circumstances only the mask, the most durable and constant portion of the costume, survives. As such, a mask may be re-animated many times, washed and repainted or anointed with sacrificial material, to be accompanied by a renewed or refreshed costume. When removed from their social and cultural context, masks rarely travel with their more fragile attachments such as feathers, plant materials or cloth costumes. Unfortunately, the great majority of the masks from Africa found in museums and collections exist in this disembodied form.

Interest has recently turned to identifying individuals who created African art, but this is no longer possible for almost all objects now in collections and museums. Although the identity of the carver of a mask was known to at least some members of an African community, explorers, scholars, and collectors until recently had no interest in this information, and it was rarely recorded. In the society where he worked, the identity of the carver was often subsidiary to the power of the objects he created or to the chief in whose court he worked. Additionally, many carvers had other occupations such as smithing, healing and divination for which they may have been better known.

The Making of African Masks

Wood is the material usually associated with African masks. Most wooden masks are carved from a single piece of lightweight, naturally white or cream-colored timber. Over many years the unfinished surfaces of these woods darken through a process of oxidation, but almost always the exposed surfaces are stained with natural pigments extracted from plants or soil, libations, or with commercially available materials such as shoe polish or paints. The original light color of the wood is revealed when the finished surface is damaged or drying causes the wood to crack.

The visibility and expressive character of masks may be enhanced by the use of bright colors and the application of shiny brass, copper, or aluminum sheets, wire, or tacks. Cloth may be incorporated into or attached to the mask, sometimes stretched over a wire frame, or the entire mask may consist only of cloth. Leather is also sometimes used in constructing a mask. Masks made entirely of metal, such as iron, copper, or brass are uncommon. Ivory masks are rare. Finally, there is a genre of masks created from ephemeral components such as grass, leaves, cloth, and other fragile materials that deteriorate rapidly or are sometimes purposefully allowed to decay or are burned after use.

Materials attached to African masks to enhance their power and attractiveness include nails, tacks, coins, bells, shells (especially cowries), beads, seeds such as red *Abrus precatorius* seeds, plant fibers, bird feathers, animal and human hair, animal claws or teeth (i.e. leopard), and porcupine quills, to name but a few of the embellishments.

Most African carvers use a small number of basic manual tools, including adzes of various types and sizes, knives, chisels, hammers, and iron tools to burn or smooth surfaces, or to make holes. The tools are endowed with sacred power that is recognized and honored in sacrificial rituals performed by the carver before he begins work. These instruments may be inherited by a leading pupil upon the death of a master carver.

Wooden masks are carved from segments of carefully selected tree trunks after the trees have been felled and allowed to dry. Having chosen a block of the appropriate size, the carver uses an adze to create the mask's basic shape that is then refined with knives and chisels. Prior to the availability of files and sandpaper, leaves with rough surfaces were used for smoothing. Holes for attaching the mask to the performer and to the costume are created at the edges of masks with a pointed awl or a red-hot poker. Further drying of the wood to inhibit cracking and improve resistance to insects is sometimes achieved by hanging masks in the rafters of a dwelling or shed where they are exposed to smoke. Over time, this results in a blackened surface. Oil and other plant material rubbed on the surface to protect the wood also imparts a dark patina with age. These traditional methods of finishing masks have in part been supplanted by the use of commercial stains, dyes, polishes, and paint. Although the majority of masks made for and used in traditional masquerades have a blackened or black-brown patina, masks colored with pigments from natural and commercial sources have been part of long-standing masking traditions. In recent circumstances, color has increasingly been used to enhance the beauty and visibility of African masks. Hence, the presence of vivid colors is not necessarily an attribute of decorative masks made only for sale.

As observed by Paul Guillaume and Thomas Munro in their 1926 book, *Primitive Negro Sculpture*, traditional African masks "...are not made in play, or in response to a pure impulse to create aesthetic forms, but as necessary instruments in the social and religious life of the tribe.... To feel the association which ... (the mask)...had for its makers, we must see how it entered into their activities." African masks are essentially utilitarian objects created for a specific purpose. Possessing magical powers, they are stored out of sight and seen only in performance on special occasions.

African Mask Performances (Masquerades)

The circumstances under which African masks perform are varied. They appear singly, in pairs, and sometimes in groups. The imagery of the mask is designed to express and reinforce the context in which it appears. Masquerades occur during daylight, at dusk, and at night. They are involved with fertility, myths of heroes and ancestors, secret society rites, healing, divination rituals, initiation ceremonies, social control, and guidance, education, funerals, weddings, protection against witchcraft, entertainment, political rallies, and various celebrations such as those preceding planting or following a harvest. Music, consisting mainly of rhythms created by drums and whistles as well as dance, acrobatics, and singing in various proportions animate performances of maskers, who may themselves utter words or sounds and contribute to the rhythm by wearing bells or carrying rattles. Depending on the particular spirit or spirits being evoked, some masked performances are stately parades, others involve choreographed dancing, and still others appear to be composed of less predictable movements or combinations of these formats. Ultimately, the totality of the performance is the result of collaboration between the maker of the mask, the wearer of the mask (who is sometimes also the maker), assistants who accompany the mask and may have helped make the costume, ritual leaders, musicians who create rhythms that modulate the intensity of the fantasy and conjure up spirits, members of the audience who may become active participants, and the response of the audience as a whole.

Masked performances have played a central role in the social, religious, cultural, and political life of African peoples for many centuries, particularly those inhabiting the Central and Western regions of the continent. Coincidentally, masquerades also provide entertainment. Upon donning the costume, the African masker is imbued with a spiritual force or is actually transformed and becomes one with the spirit represented by the mask. Western comic book characters such as Batman and Robin exemplify the same process of mask and costume-associated transformation that endows the masker with supernatural powers. The masked performer becomes the embodiment of a transcendental spiritual force or supernatural being.

The role that masking plays in Africa is analogous to that of puppetry and the converse of the widespread perception that donning a mask is an act of deception, disguise, and concealment. It is therefore noteworthy that the firmly established *Sogo Bò* puppetry tradition in Mali includes masked performers as well as puppets without making a distinction between the two genres.

The way the mask is intended to appear to the audience and the reaction it is expected to elicit are reflected in the design of the mask and costume. The interaction between masker and onlookers depends, in large part, upon traditions that evolved over time. Some masquerades continue with little change for years, but others are revised or abandoned, and new masquerades are introduced from time to time. When masquerades have been performed repeatedly, the audience often knows what to expect and how to respond. The majority of African masks are associated directly or indirectly with spirits, supernatural beings, or animals. They may refer to particular events, but they only rarely depict specific individuals. The masked figure is viewed by the audience as constituting a visit by the spirit from "the beyond" or spirit world. In this context, the spirits may be those of ancestors, mythical persons, animals, or inanimate natural objects. Some masks may represent more than one spirit so that the entire masquerade, including the costume and music, is required to determine the precise subject of the performance.

The special importance of ancestors in African masquerades is a consequence of the fact that social life throughout most of Africa centers around the family and village. Showing reverence for and maintaining good relations with the spirits of the ancestors is considered to be essential for community harmony, prosperity, and health. Ancestors are respected and feared because of the profound role their spirits are believed to play in the life of the individual, the family, and the community. The family is the traditional social and economic unit in which seniority is the basis of the authority of elders who are responsible for the family's welfare. Longevity is viewed as an indication that the spirits of those who are already ancestors look favorably upon the elders, who are themselves soon to become ancestors. In this context, the word ancestors refers not only to dead members of a family lineage but also to deceased important members of the community.

Individual ancestors of high status are only infrequently depicted in a semi-naturalistic rendering as a mask, statue, or shrine. Generic, abstract, or representational forms with various embellishments are most often used. Non-ancestral spirits that inhabit the forest and bush outside the village are typically presented in the form of animal masquerades. Bold, fantastical, and unnatural masks often represent spirits, mythical characters, or animals associated with the origins of a people. Masks with a serene appearance typically embody ancestors and magic cults. The non-human nature of a spirit manifested by a masquerade is often emphasized by a voluminous, abstract outfit that completely disguises the performer and focuses attention on the mask. Raffia, leaves, grass, corn stalks, other plant materials, and cloth may be used to create these costumes. Some costumes are ornamented with shells, mirrors, beads, bells, amulets, ribbons, and other objects. Other masquerades, such as those of the Chokwe in Democratic of Congo, reveal the human form of the masker who wears a close-fitting outfit of specially created, heavy netting.

Masks from West and Central Africa

Africa

FOREHEAD MASK (Dugn'be)
Bidjogo People: Guinea Bissau *(Bissagos Islands)*
Materials: *Wood, cow horns, glass, rope, pigment. H 7 in. W 19 in.*

The cow or bull mask *(dugn'be)* represents an impulsive, uneducated youth. It is worn by an adolescent boy of the preinitiatory *canhocá* grade indicating the end of childhood. The cord through the nostrils is an allusion to a similarly placed rope used to control a calf until it has matured and been tamed. The mask is worn on top of the head with the face pointing upward except when the masker mimics the behavior of a cow or bull while crawling on all fours. A larger mask is worn by initiates in their late teens and twenties *(cabaros)*. It represents a wild bull *(vaca bruto)*, with a ribbed neck and a protruding red tongue. The dancer wears decorative arm bands, a raffia skirt, and ankle rattles. He may also carry a sword or stick. After the wearer has passed initiation and is considered an adult, the mask is no longer worn.

Fig. 1

BODY MASK
Bidjogo People: Guinea Bissau *(Bissagos Islands)*
Materials: *Wood, rope, foam rubber, pigment, nails. H 9 in.*

This unusual body mask is worn on the performer's back and held in place by the attached ropes. It is a representation of the cow or bull whose head appears as the *dugbn'be* mask during initiation ceremonies for boys.

Fig. 2

Fig. 3

BODY MASK
Bidjogo People: Guinea Bissau *(Bissagos Islands)*
Materials: *Wood, pigment.*
H 24.5 in.

In addition to the cow and bull, aquatic animals, such as the shark and swordfish, are represented in some Bidjogo initiation ceremonies. The shark-related regalia includes a shark-shaped fish worn on the top of the head. A representation of the dorsal fin shown here is tied to the dancer's back or shoulder. The fin is decorated on both sides with various carved and painted aquatic motifs of symbolic significance to the Bidjogo people. These include a sea turtle, a hammerhead shark, a pelican, and a mermaid-like female figure with a serpentine tail, possibly a reference to Mami Wata. The performance, consisting of dance, music and song, celebrates the initiate's prowess as a fisherman.

Fig. 4

Fig. 5

Fig. 6

Fig. 7

HEADDRESS MASKS *(Bansonyi)*
Baga People: Guinea
Materials: *Wood, pigment.* Fig. 5: *H 52 in.;* Figs. 6 & 7: *H 54 in.*

The snake masks (*a-Mantsho-na-Tshol* or *Bansonyi*, the Master of Medicine) of the Baga, Nalu, and Landuma people embody the snake spirit that is associated with fertility, prosperity, and protection from danger. The mask represents the venerated, mythical serpent, *Ninkinanka*, who guided their ancestors to the region they currently inhabit and protected them en route. The mask is sometimes decorated with mirrors, ribbons, feathers, and small bells. Placed in a receptacle in a conical armature made of palm fronds that is supported by the dancer's shoulders, the snake towers above the performer's head. A costume of textiles or palm fibers hanging from the framework covers the performer. *Ninkinanka* is associated with rainbows, a metaphor for the beginning and the end. It is the source of rain, wealth, and fertility. The *Bansonyi* mask appears as a protective spirit at male initiation ceremonies in which adolescent boys are taught secrets of the snake spirit.

The 54-inch tall, more colorful and sinuous snake **(Fig. 6)** has a peg at the bottom that fits into a hollow receptacle at the apex of the supporting armature. It is Janus-headed with faces on the front and back. The chevron and diamond-shaped carved and painted motifs are typical for this type of headdress mask.

The 52-inch tall, straight snake **(Fig. 5)** is the older of the pair. The single face is defined by slightly raised round eyes. A carved ridge and a diamond-shaped motif extend along the front surface. Remnants of layers of paint can be appreciated on the surface. The concave base would sit like a cap on the dancer's padded head held in place by an armature.

Fig. 8

HEADDRESS MASK
(D'mba-Da-Tshol)
Baga People: Guinea
Materials: *Wood, pigment.*
H 28 in.

This extremely rare female bust headdress is worn on top of the head with the stem at the base attached to a supporting framework that is covered by the dancer's costume. The deformed bust, with only one eye, ear, and breast, represents the opposite of the beautiful woman. The masker wears a disheveled outfit of torn rags, leaves, and grain bags. She is a fool, a beggar, and an undisciplined woman whose antics both amuse and frighten the crowd of onlookers. This mask is owned by the community elders and appears during transitional stages of life such as funerals, where it serves to distract the bereaved family and relieve tension as well as at weddings and initiation rites.

Fig. 9

FACE MASK *(Landa)*
Toma (Loma) People: Guinea
Materials: *Wood, metal, pigment. H 13 in.*

These masks are used by members of the *Poro* Society. Characteristic features are the flat face, a domed forehead with a sharp brow, and the angular nose. The mask illustrated here has projecting, tubular eyes that serve to disguise the small, round eyeholes. Metal strips have been added to the face, and there are metal discs at the ends of the tubular eyes. Before the metal became tarnished it would have gleamed brightly during a performance.

BODY MASK
Koranko People:
Guinea; Sierra Leone
Materials: *Wood, raffia, cloth, beads, mirror, medicine packet.*
H 20.5 in.

Worn on the back, this type of mask was used during initiation into the secret men's *Poro* Society, and it was restricted to the sacred forest where these rites were performed. The rear surface of the mask is flat, a feature consistent with this usage. The blunt, minimally tapered horns with a rectangular cross-section are characteristic of a Koranko *Poro* mask. Red, a color associated with *Poro*, is represented by the red beads on the surface of the medicine packet that contains "magical" substances. Part of a mirror is also evident. The medicine packet and mirror serve as protective amulets. A *Poro* mask endows the wearer with the power of a bush spirit involved in the secret initiation rites of the *Poro* Society. The three grades of initiation are boys, men, and elders. The presence of four horns on this mask suggests that it belongs to the intermediate or men's grade.

Fig. 10

Fig. 11

HEADDRESS MASK (*Gbetu*)
Gola People: Liberia
Materials: *Wood, metal, pigment. H 27 in.*

This casque-type mask consists of a bowl-shaped, hollow helmet base giving rise to a central column that is topped by a female head. The helmet component has incised rectangular designs that probably represent protective amulets. The neck is ringed, the eyes of the female head at the top of the column are accentuated by metal inserts, and the helmet component is adorned by dime-sized metal discs arranged in a ring around the base of the neck.

These masks belong to and are danced by men at funerals, holidays, and in rituals associated with the men's *Poro* Society. A voluminous costume of raffia fibers hides small children dressed in raffia who come and go from beneath the skirt like chicks with a mother hen. The mask is considered to be feminine because it appears to give birth to the children.

The drama of the Gola masquerade is captured in the following description recorded by Esther Warner in her book, *New Song in a Strange Land*:

...the Play Devil entered with a great fanfare of wooden horns and bells. He wore a long-necked black mask which reached down over his head to his shoulders. His costume was layers and layers of raffia, so that he resembled an animated haystack... He was the height of two men when he entered, but at moments of great activity he would suddenly shrink to ordinary height, then become tall again. He turned somersaults and cartwheels. Finally he sank in the dust, a weary heap of grass, rose again, and whirled away like a tumbleweed.

FACE MASK
Dan People: Liberia; Ivory Coast
Materials: *Wood, pigment.* Fig. 12: *H 9 in.*; Fig. 13: *H 9 in.*

The traditional blackened face masks of the Dan people are used in rituals of the secret men's *Poro* Society. Worn by men, the masks participate in many *Poro* functions involved in maintaining community stability. Unadorned masks of the Dan people have a smooth, shiny blackened surface. Masks with masculine attributes have large, round eyes **(Fig. 12)** whereas those considered to be feminine have narrow, slit-shaped eyes **(Fig. 13)**. The eyes of a masculine mask may be encircled by metal strips, and these masks often display teeth. The forehead is typically rounded and bulging, and it may have a central, raised vertical "scarification." The spirit of the mask is sometimes "activated" by hammering a nail into the forehead. The nail is sometimes bent, and when the mask is "retired" the nail may be removed leaving a hole in the forehead. The role played by a Dan mask may change over time as the mask ascends in the hierarchy of masquerades.

The appearance of a masked Dan dancer is captured by Ladislas Segy in the following description from his book, *Masks of Black Africa*:

The dancer appeared fully dressed wearing a typical black, Dan-style mask...a blue blouse richly embroidered with red, yellow and green designs, and a raffia skirt. His legs, feet, and hands were fully covered according to ancient tradition so as to not show any part of the natural body, the masked dancer supposedly representing a nonhuman spirit.

Fig. 12

Fig. 13

Fig. 14

Fig. 15

FACE MASKS *(Zakpai Or Ge)*
Dan People: Liberia; Ivory Coast
Materials: *Wood, cloth, metal, raffia, pigment.*
Fig. 14: *H 18 in.;* Fig. 15: *H 9.5 in.*

These masculine masks are entirely covered by red cloth **(Fig. 15)** or they feature a red cloth band across the open, round eyes **(Fig. 14)**. The masks have beards and moustaches that are indications of higher ancestral status. Red cloth imparts aggressive meaning to the mask. A hole in the forehead of the mask covered with red cloth is the site where a nail that activated the power or spirit of the mask had been removed after the mask was "retired." Shiny metal rings and strips around the eyes of the mask with a red band across the face accentuate the mask's fierce mien and may have been intended to divert viewers from seeing the dancer's eyes. The eyes of the mask covered by red cloth were probably encircled by metal rings that are now lost, leaving only the adhesive material that held them in place.

Zakpai masks are worn by teams of men representing forest spirits or *Ge,* who compete in races against teams of unmasked men. Similar masks are also worn by men acting as "fire wardens," who check cooking fires in the community to prevent them from getting out of control and causing a village conflagration, especially during the windy, dry season. The costume includes cloth over the head and a body covering of cloth and raffia.

Fig. 16

Fig. 17

HELMET MASK
(Deangle Or Takangle)
Dan People: Liberia; Ivory Coast
Materials: *Wood, plant fibers, cloth, cowrie shells, pigment, bells. H 12 in. W 22 in.*

Masks with this elaborate helmet component were used primarily for entertainment. In this instance, the mask has feminine facial features characterized by narrow, slit-shaped eyes. Note the medicine packet situated on the head of the mask just behind the corona of cowrie shells. This mask is a contemporary replica of a traditional form.

Fig. 18

Fig. 19

FACE MASKS *(Kaogle)*
Dan People: Liberia; Ivory Coast
Materials: *Wood, pigment, metal, fur.* Fig. 18: *H 9.5 in.;* Fig. 19: *H 10 in.*

The prominent, triangular cheekbones of the *Kaogle* mask are a reference to simian features of the chimpanzee character it represents. In contrast to orderly community life resulting from positive human attributes such as ritual and cooperation, the performance of the *Kaogle* mask serves as a warning against the unpredictable, destructive behavior associated with the animalistic aspects of human nature. This point is brought home to the crowd of onlookers by violent actions such as throwing hooked sticks at them. One mask has a bent nail in the forehead, fur around the mouth, representing a beard and moustache, and a single, wooden tooth **(Fig. 18)**. The raised, central, vertical design element on the forehead of the other mask probably represents a scarification **(Fig. 19)**.

FACE MASK
Ngere (We) People: Liberia; Ivory Coast
Materials: *Wood, bells, cloth, pigment, wool. H 12 in.*

This mask with slit-shaped eyes and multiple bells is worn by a man who sings songs accompanied by dance and music. The masquerade acts as a griot who tells stories, recites poems, and praises members of the community. These performances maintain cultural history among the We-speaking people. The mask is also worn when disputes are settled and in some other circumstances. In performance, the mask is surmounted by an elongated cloth cap that is decorated with cowrie shells and a knee-length raffia cloak. As is true of with many Dan masks, the function of the mask and its level in the masquerade hierarchy depend on the complexity of the entire costume, the music, the words recited, and the dances that are performed. Over time and in the course of multiple performances, a Dan mask may rise stepwise in stature. The distressed surface of the mask reveals multiple layers of colorful paint.

Fig. 20

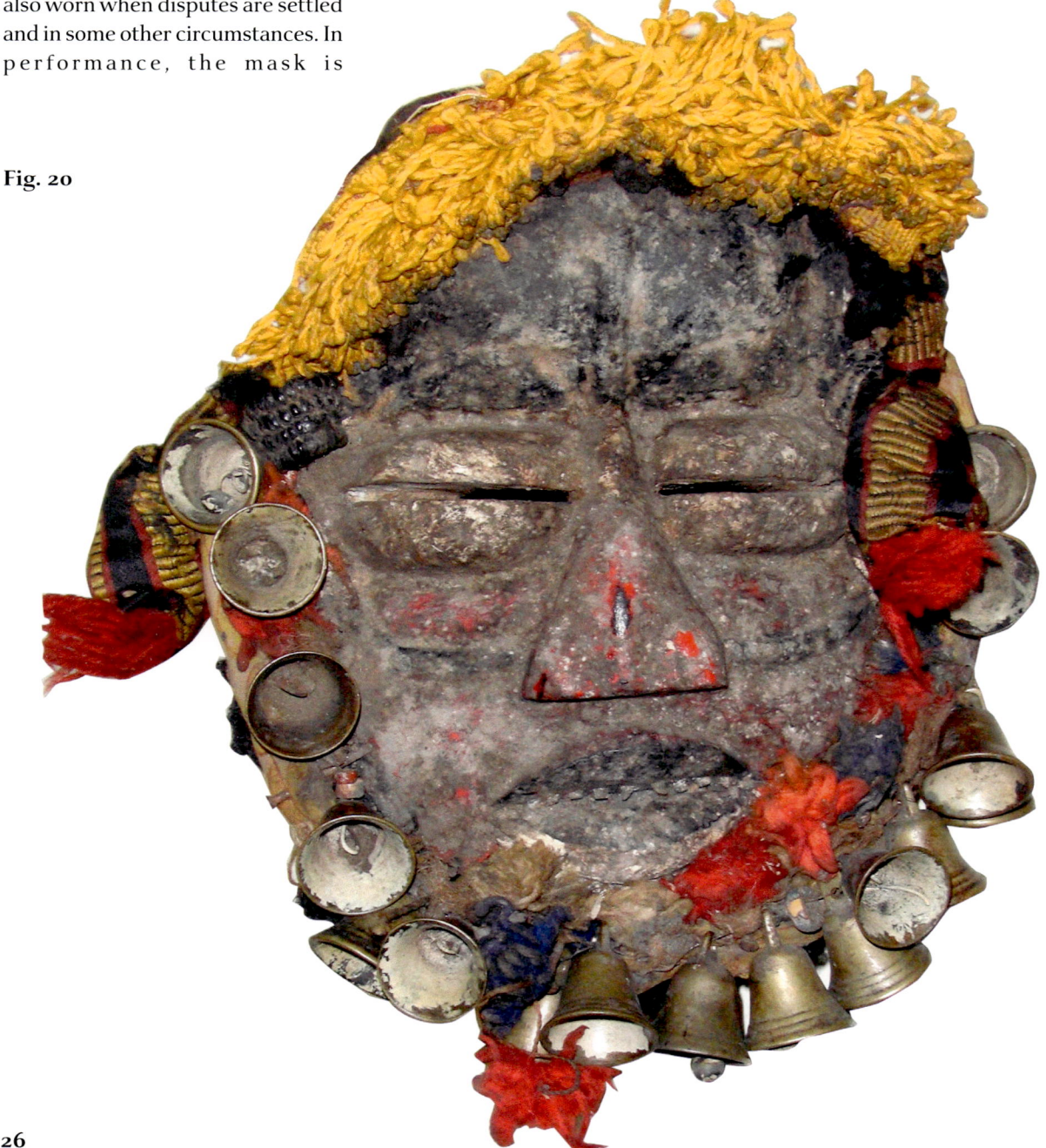

Fig. 21

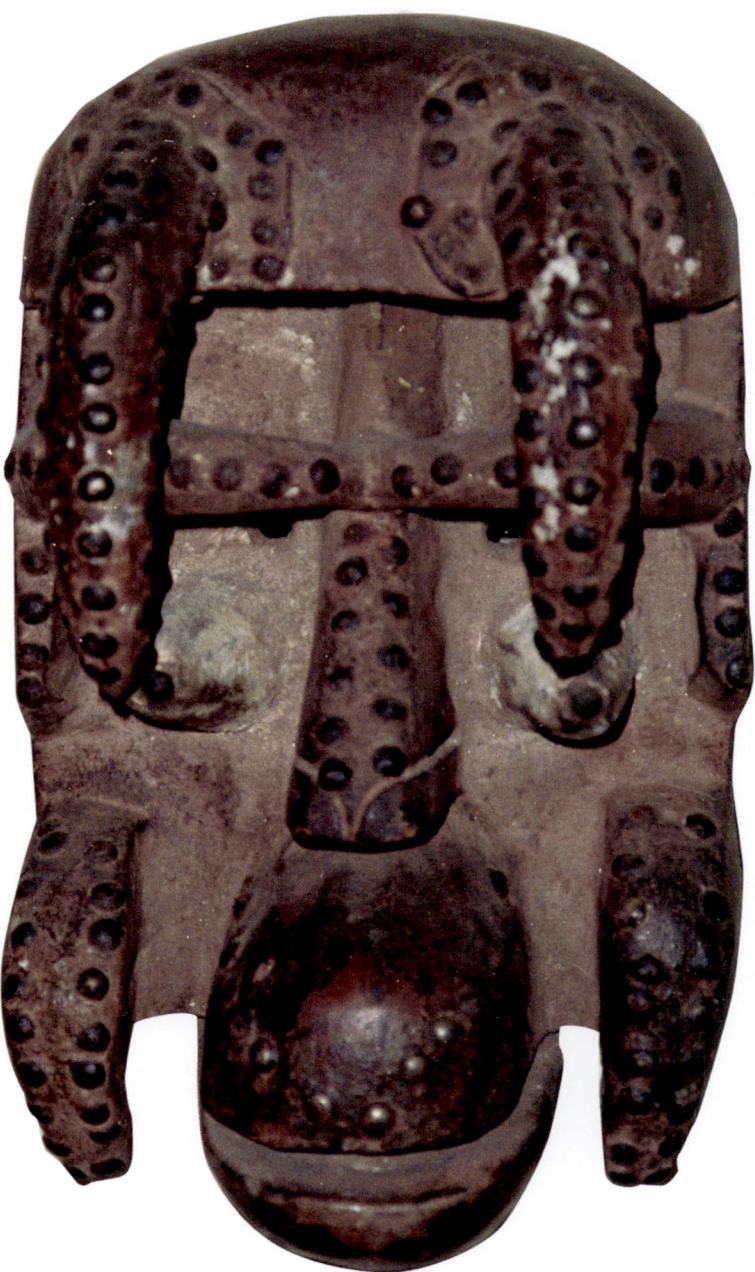

FACE MASK (*Gla*)
Bete People: Liberia; Ivory Coast
Materials: *Wood, metal tacks, pigment. H 13.5 in.*

This aggressive appearing, fierce mask with tubular eyes, an articulated jaw and multiple, prominent horns is decorated with brass tacks that add to the power of the mask. Just below each of the eyeholes there is a kaolin-whitened, conical protrusion tipped with a brass tack. As is the case with the previously illustrated Toma *Landa* mask, these structural features are probably intended to protect the wearer from malevolent spirits and supernatural forces.

These masks were danced at funerals and by judges seeking persons accused of misdeeds or "witchcraft." They were also worn by warriors to frighten enemies during battle. In contemporary society, *Gla* masks appear at civic events to protect against threats to community harmony.

Fig. 22

FACE MASK
Kru (Grebo) People: Liberia; Ivory Coast
Materials: *Wood, pigment, plant fibers. H 27 in.*

The multiple pairs of tubular eyes that characterize this mask reflect the mask's ability to see forces and spirits that are not visible to ordinary persons. By wearing this mask, the performer was endowed with supernatural, clairvoyant powers. In performance, the mask was attached to a wicker framework, part of which remains on the back of this example. Small, round holes between the lower two pairs of tubular eyes permitted the masker to see where he was going. Masks of this type were sometimes placed in front of the chief's house as a sign of authority.

Many of these masks were decorated with bird feathers placed into holes in the top edge. Only stubs of broken feathers remain attached to this example. This mask is unusual because it has a beak-like extension instead of a rectangular mouth at the lower end. This feature, as well as the tubular eyes, supports the hypothesis that the form of this type of Kru mask has features in common with masks worn on the forehead or on top of the head by the Ijo people of Nigeria with whom the Kru people had contact when they served as sailors aboard British ships in the 19th century. Referring to Ijo masks, GI Jones has suggested that Kru sailors "...could have taken some of the masks back with them and had them copied in their home village."

Fig. 23

FACE MASKS *(Kplekplé)*
Baule People: Ivory Coast
Materials: *Wood, pigment.* Fig. 24: *H 13.5 in.;* Fig. 25: *H 16 in.*

The *Kplekplé* mask is one of a group of masks that participate in masquerades of the *Goli* Society at funerals, for entertainment, or when the community is threatened by natural forces such as famine or drought. They appear in pairs during the day at the start of the ceremony. One of the paired masks is red (usually female) and the other is black (usually male), a reference to family and marriage. The *Goli* masquerade consists of a series of dances that trace the transition from the foolish, willful, aggressive behavior of youth and spirits of the bush to the civilized conduct of a family and orderly village that comes with maturity. *Kplekplé*, playfully and vigorously danced by boys, is the first of the mask sequences to appear. In performance, the mask has a fringe of palm fronds that form part of the dancer's costume as well as metal anklets that jingle as he moves and an animal skin attached to his back.

Both of the illustrated masks are the red, female type. The semi-lunar horns with nearly touching tips, tubular eyes above inverted, triangular eye holes and the rectangular mouth are characteristic features of the *Kplekplé* mask. The motifs at the bases of the horns of the 13.5-inch tall mask suggest ears **(Fig. 24)**, whereas the crescent on the forehead of the 16-inch tall mask might refer to the Islamic crescent moon **(Fig. 25)**. The deeper of the two masks **(Fig. 25)** was stabilized on the wearer's face by a small rod across the inside that the dancer held with his teeth.

Fig. 24

Fig. 25

Fig. 26

HELMET MASK *(Kponyungo, Waniugo)*
Senufo People: Ivory Coast
Materials: *Wood, pigment. H 11.5 in. W 32 in.*

The *Kponyungo*, or fire-spitter mask is a composite, zoomorphic creation representing multiple animals of spiritual significance to the Senufo people, including the horns of an antelope, a chameleon, a hornbill bird, the tusks of a warthog, and the mouth of a carnivore such as the hyena or crocodile. A receptacle for magical substances may be part of the mask or it can be attached to the performer's costume. By blowing into hot coals held in front of the mask or placed in the mouth of the mask, the performer can make it appear that the mask is spitting fire. The entire assemblage is intended to convey the concept of a savage creature that has the power to protect against the danger and chaos posed by sorcery practiced by hidden witches. Together with the tortoise, python, and crocodile, the chameleon and hornbill bird are primordial animals in Senufo mythology. The hornbill bird, a representative of the ancestors, transmits knowledge through the chameleon to the wearer of the mask. These masks belong to the *Poro* Society and appear in groups at funeral ceremonies for society members to facilitate the passage of the soul of the deceased to the spirit world.

Fig. 27

PLANK MASK (*Bedu*)
Nfana People: Ivory Coast; Ghana
Materials: *Wood, pigment. H 43 in.*

These large masks **(Fig. 28)** fashioned from a single plank belong to the *Bedu* Society that arose in the late 1920s in the Bondoukou region of the Ivory Coast. The *Bedu* Society stresses the importance of strong community and family ties as expressed in song and dance. The maskers appear singly or as male/female pairs at funeral and harvest festivals to ward off evil and to encourage family and community unity. The masks may be several feet tall and weigh as much as 100 pounds. The male mask is topped by horns, a reference to the buffalo. Female masks have a round superstructure with a central aperture.

Fig. 28

Fig. 29

FACE MASK (*Yangaleya*)
Ligbi People:
Ivory Coast; Ghana
Materials: *Wood, pigment. H 13 in.*

The *Yangaleya* mask **(Fig. 29)** represents the hornbill, a bird with a powerful beak and mythical qualities for many African peoples. The hornbill looks after the souls of the dead and is a symbol of fertility for members of the *Do* Society. The paired *Yangaleya* maskers perform a graceful dance in unison.

FACE OR HELMET MASK (*Aron Arabai*)
Temne People: Sierra Leone
Materials: *Brass, cloth.* Fig. 30: *H 10.5;* Fig. 31: *H 10.5;* Fig. 32: *H 13 in.*

Three examples of the *Aron arabai* type of mask are illustrated. These rare masks are only worn by a man who represents the alter ego or guardian spirit *(Karfi)* of the chief and his clan. Faces such as these were sometimes attached to leather helmet masks or they were perched tilted at an acute angle on the wearer's forehead. The masks are cut and shaped from thin copper or brass sheets with hammered, repoussé and punched decorative designs. Ears are typically attached as separate pieces. The dancer is concealed by a raffia or a country cloth costume.

The elaborate repoussé work on one mask consists of complex scrollwork over the face and a design that appears to be composed of symbols from an alphabet across the forehead **(Fig. 30)**. A shroud made from traditional, hand woven, country strip cloth with brown and beige stripes is tightly bound to the mask with linear, paired repoussé scarifications on the forehead, cheeks, and corners of the mouth **(Fig. 31)**. Sierra Leone one-cent and twenty-cent coins from the 1960s are attached around the perimeter of the largest mask, and the circumference of the face is decorated with circular, repoussé designs that resemble large versions of the coins **(Fig. 32)**. The dentate upper edge of this mask suggests hair or the rays of the sun.

Fig. 30

Fig. 31

Fig. 32

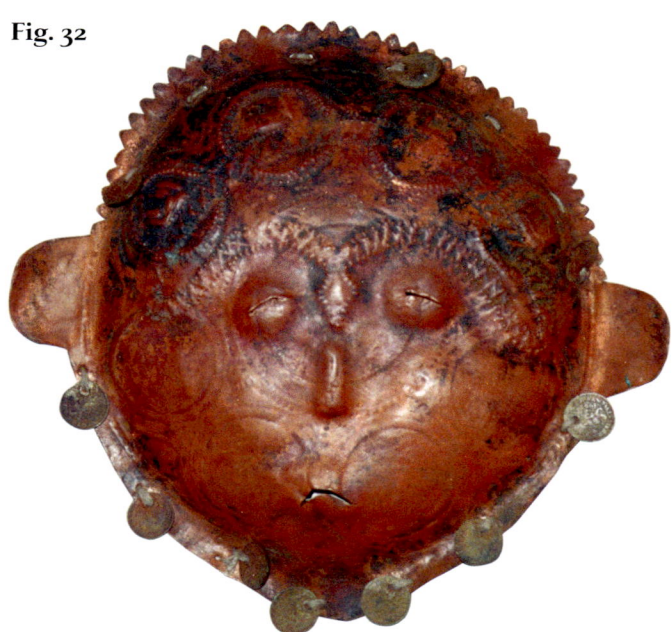

HELMET MASK
Limba People: Sierra Leone
Materials: *Copper. H 9 in.*

This rare Janus chief's helmet mask, attributed to the Limba people, is made from joined thin sheets of copper. Holes for the eyes and mouth have been punched through the metal. The faces, having different expressions on the front and back, are outlined by strings of repoussé dots, and repoussé folds simulate neck rings around the lower half of the helmet. This mask may have had the same function in relation to the installation and authority of chiefs as the previously illustrated *aron arabai* masks of the Temne people.

Fig. 33

The Sande Society in Sierra Leone and Liberia

The *Sande* or *Bundu* Society is the most important women's association of all major ethnic groups in Sierra Leone and the Bassa region of Liberia. It is concerned mainly with the initiation of girls and young women, a rite that is traditionally carried out in a secluded bush camp outside the village over a period of several weeks to months. During this time, the girls are trained to be responsible wives and mothers through instruction in rituals, songs, dance, crafts, and discipline. The entire process is organized and implemented by members of the *Bundu* Society under a leader or *digba,* who is imbued with special knowledge and wisdom imparted to her by the ancestors. This knowledge is embodied in a female figure *(minsere* or *min si le)* representing female ancestors. The authority of the *digba* depends on guidance she receives from the *minsere*.

Sowei masks are insignia of the *digba* and other senior members of the *Sande* Society. They appear at various stages during the initiation and are worn by members of the society who serve as intermediaries between the village and the bush initiation camp. *Nowo* is a female spirit who appears wearing the *sowei* mask. She represents beauty, proper comportment, and leadership. The masks and raffia costumes are blackened, since black is associated with the orderly, known world in contrast to white representing the supernatural.

Sowei masks are said to be created by water spirits and to come from under the water. They may be stored in a lake or stream near a village. The significance of the neck rings found on the masks is controversial, but one interpretation is that they symbolize ripples created in the water as the mask emerges. The rings are also associated with a healthy, well-fed woman.

As reported by Frederick Lamp in his book, *African Art of the West Atlantic Coast,* "(the)...Mende affirm that they do not expect perfect female beauty in this human life on earth, that perfect beauty is divine, unearthly from paradise, and thus can only be imagined." According to Sylvia Ardyn Boone in *Radiance from the Waters: Ideals of Feminine Beauty in Mende Art*, for the *Sande* society the "definition of beauty is concerned more with care given to one's appearance than God-given physical form. A woman who possesses aesthetically fine features but who neglects the maintenance of her hair and body is not considered beautiful." As a consequence, the face of a *sowei* mask is stylized with specific features de-emphasized. The ears, mouth and nose are small, and the chin is pointed. The narrow eyes are usually closed, and the masker looks through slits below the eyes or in the neck. Particular attention is paid to sculpting the coiffure that may incorporate amulets, cowries, coins, seeds, animal horns, and combs worn by *Sande* initiates in their hair. Small duiker antelope horns usually appear in the coiffure as multiples in rows, whereas horns of sheep and cows are paired.

A white cloth was usually tied around a sculpted prominence on top of the mask. The least complex of these supports are one or more knobs. Various animals and inanimate objects may also be found on top of *sowei* masks, such as a turtle (a water-dwelling spirit), a bird (able to communicate with the spirit world), a snake (associated with water spirits or Mami Wata), hats and crowns (prestige items), amulets in a number of forms (protection against harm), or an inverted cooking pot (symbolizes rebirth during initiation when a ritual meal of rice is finished and the cooking pot is turned over). Human figures, singly, in pairs or as a foursome are less frequent on *sowei* masks than animals. The human figures function as spirits who can observe everything and warn the wearer of witchcraft.

Strips of silver or aluminum are sometimes attached to the surface of the mask to emphasize lines or to decorate the coiffure. Earrings consisting of simple copper or brass rings may be present. The blackened skin surface of the mask is intended to be smooth and shiny to reflect a robust, healthy, well-fed woman. Masks that are stored in a stream lose their shiny surface. The black pigment is renewed periodically, and it may accumulate, becoming so encrusted that the carved designs become blurred. Eventually, a mask in this condition may be adapted for use as a *gonde* or clown mask serving as the antithesis of the beautiful *sowei* mask.

Sowei Helmet Masks of Sierra Leone and Liberia

Helmet masks of the *Sande* Society are one of the few mask forms in Africa that belong to and are worn exclusively by women. In addition to the Mende people, similar masks are employed by women of the Bassa, Gola, Temne, and other peoples who inhabit areas near the Mende in Sierra Leone and Liberia. These masks are used by officials of the *Sande* Society that is responsible for the initiation of girls and young women at the time of puberty. The spirit of *Sande* that is embodied by the *sowei* mask resides under water. The process by which girls go to the initiation camp is likened to becoming immersed in water to achieve a state of perfection that is exemplified by the fine coiffure displayed by the initiates when they return.

Sowei masks are carved from the trunk of the bombax or silk cottonwood tree that produces a relatively lightweight wood. Most *sowei* masks have a single face in the front. Janus (two-faced) and four-faced *sowei* masks are uncommon. A collarette of blackened raffia is suspended from holes placed circumferentially just above the lower rim of the mask. The masker also wears a black raffia costume that covers the entire body, hands and feet **(Fig. 34)**. Early descriptions of *Bundu* maskers referred to them as "devil masks" or "bush devils."

Although the general form of the mask is stylized, each mask is individualized to reflect the owner's persona, and the mask is identified by a particular name that refers to the personality of the owner. The face of the mask is compressed to the lower half or third of the cylinder. The eyes, nose, mouth, and ears are de-emphasized. The narrow eyes are closed or barely open slits. The forehead, considered to be the seat of character, is prominent. This concept is expressed in the Mende blessing, "May God make your forehead large." Carved designs and marks present on the forehead, cheeks or at the outer corners of the eyes correspond to facial

Fig. 34

scarifications traditionally made by the specific ethnic group to which the mask belongs.

The elaborate coiffure that occupies about one third of the mask is based on one of the traditional hairstyles, consisting of ridges, lobes, buns, or tufts. Older masks usually had a series of ridges running from the front to the back. The ridges may all be of the same height or the central ridge may taller than those on either side. The number of ridges is odd because there is always a central ridge between an equal number of lateral ridges on each side. The ridges may be parallel or they may converge at a central point on the forehead and back of the head. A hairstyle composed of four lobes was more common prior to World War I, whereas six or eight lobes were more frequent in later years, particularly after World War II. Hair in each lobe was typically braided and tied in a knot.

Other forms of coiffure included hair gathered into small buns that were tied off at the top, hair arranged in many small balls, and the use of blackened raffia net as a decorative device.

The woman who commissions the mask that is created by a male carver selects the ornamental and symbolic motifs that decorate the hair. These motifs include household objects, human figures, and various animals. Snakes, turtles, and fish (animals associated with water) are chosen as intermediaries between the real world above water and the spiritual world below the water's surface. Zigzag designs may represent water. Birds, animals that inhabit the land and air, are represented because they are thought to be endowed with the ability to communicate with and transmit messages from spirits. Amulets or *lasimoisia* (sing. *lasimoi*) hung from the raffia costume or attached to the hair were used as protection against evil spirits, witchcraft, and jealousy. These consisted of Arabic text, often from the Koran, in a leather or silver packet. Representations of amulets were also carved on the top or surface of a *sowei* mask. An amulet carved on the top of a mask may be pyramidal, resemble an inverted table, or look like a book. A scrap of paper with Koranic text is sometimes placed in a hole ("medicine hole") bored into the top of the mask from the inside to serve as an invisible amulet for added protection. Animal horns carved on masks are a reference to the horns of duiker antelope, sheep, or goats that were used as traditional medicine containers to hold herbal and other ritual substances. The horns were another form of amulet to protect the wearer against witchcraft. Mirrors attached to the mask serve as amulets that ward off evil and reflect it back to the perpetrator. Old West African colonial coins on the forehead of a mask may have been used as amulets, as a sign of wealth, or simply as decorative elements. Cowrie shells, another motif that decorates *sowei* masks, are also a reference to wealth because they were a traditional form of currency.

Amulets are still widely used in West Africa, as described in the following *New York Times* report about the civil war in Ivory Coast dated March 9, 2011, from Abidjan: "Several members of the Invisible Commando… carrying weapons and giving orders were in evidence at the check points Tuesday. They wore amulets, bracelets or trinkets that residents here said carried magic powers…"

Fig. 35

HELMET MASK (*Sowei*)
Mende People: Sierra Leone
Materials: *Wood, pigment, metal. H 16 in.*

The four seated female figures on top of this mask represent an extraordinary feat of carving since the entire mask **(Fig. 35)** was created from a single block of wood. Gazing slightly upward, the seated women act as guardians looking out for danger that could come from any direction. Carved creases at the corners of the eyes and eyebrows that radiate from the upper eyelids give the face of the helmet portion of the mask a particularly expressive appearance. Slit-shaped apertures in the eyes provide visibility for the wearer. There is a small, silver-colored wire earring in the mask's right ear lobe.

HELMET MASK (*Sowei*)
Mende People: Sierra Leone
Materials: *Wood, pigment. H 17.5 in.*

The single female figure situated on the crown of this mask **(Fig. 36)** has her arms raised and her hands behind her head. She serves as a spirit guarding the wearer of the mask.

Fig. 36

Fig. 37

Fig. 38

HELMET MASK (*Sowei*)
Mende People: Sierra Leone
Materials: *Wood, pigment.*
H 19 in.

Two female figures appear on the upper part of this mask. In front, above the face, the bust of a woman with upraised arms holds a trunk with a lock on top of her head with both hands. There is a bracelet on her right wrist. In the rear of the head, there is the full figure of a seated woman with her knees thrust upward. Her raised arms are rotated behind her head, and the hands are separated by a space as wide as the trunk held by the woman in the front. The coiffure between the figures is divided into four lobes.

Fig. 39

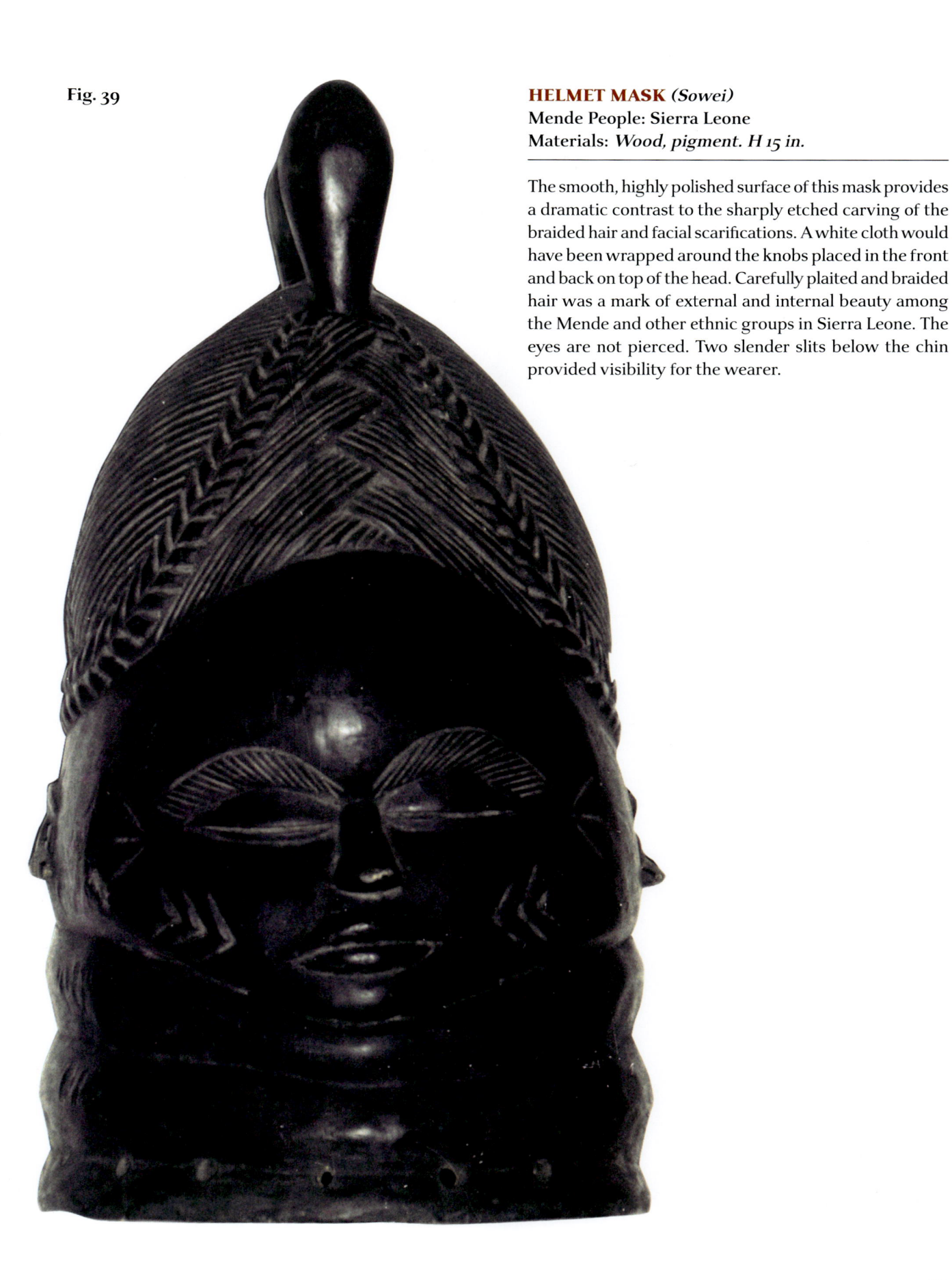

HELMET MASK (*Sowei*)
Mende People: Sierra Leone
Materials: *Wood, pigment. H 15 in.*

The smooth, highly polished surface of this mask provides a dramatic contrast to the sharply etched carving of the braided hair and facial scarifications. A white cloth would have been wrapped around the knobs placed in the front and back on top of the head. Carefully plaited and braided hair was a mark of external and internal beauty among the Mende and other ethnic groups in Sierra Leone. The eyes are not pierced. Two slender slits below the chin provided visibility for the wearer.

Fig. 40

HELMET MASK (*Sowei*)
Sherbro People: Sierra Leone
Materials: *Wood, pigment.*
H 16 in.

The carefully plaited coiffure of this beautifully carved mask is held in place by strands of carved cowrie shells that descend from a pair of top knots to a band across the forehead and in the rear to above the ears. The hair is also gathered into braids that hang in front of the ears. In the rear the hair hangs in eight braids that terminate in round knobs that may represent knots or beads. Scarifications appear on *sowei* masks for decorative purposes, but they are based on traditional designs. Carved motifs that decorate the forehead include a rosette on each side, flanking a central rectangle divided into small squares that is a characteristic of Sherbro *sowei* masks. Vertical scarifications on both cheeks are "tear marks" *(ngaya maki)*. Three lines radiating from the corners of the eyes *(kesi)* represent scarifications produced by incisions in children to allow "poisoned blood" to escape. Horizontal slits perforate the eyes.

Fig. 41

Fig. 42

HELMET MASK (*Sowei*)
Mende People: Sierra Leone
Materials: *Wood, pigment, metal. H 15.5 in.*

The proportions of this *Bundu* mask are unusual because the face is placed in the middle rather than in the lower third of the frontal plane. Neck rings occupy the entire lower third of the mask. The forehead is framed above by a carved string of cowrie shells, and the carefully plaited hair is held in place by a comb-like device. Small, metal stud earrings are present. The dull patina is a result of the mask having been submerged in water where it was protected from insects and drying. Storage in water also had symbolic significance because *sowei* masks are associated with the world of spirits beneath the water. Before use, the mask would be brought to a shiny patina with pigment and oil.

HELMET MASK *(Sowei)*
Mende People: Sierra Leone
Materials: *Wood, pigment, metal, raffia. H 15 in.*

The coiffure of this mask is divided into four lobes that are drawn together in a large knot on top and into several small knots around the perimeter. Silver-colored metal strips accentuate the carved bands separating the hair lobes. Similar metal strips form a ring connecting the small hair knots around the large, central topknot. The topknot is hollow with a small, partially occluded hole in the top through which "medicine" may have been inserted. No interior medicine hole connecting with the topknot is evident. Metal inserts highlight scarifications. The eyes are perforated by wide, slender horizontal slits. A voluminous ruff of black raffia fibers obscures the neck rings.

Fig. 43

HELMET MASK *(Sowei)*
Mende People: Sierra Leone
Materials: *Wood, pigment, raffia. H 14.5 in.*

The lobed coiffure of this mask is drawn into a large, central hair knot and smaller knots in front and back. Pointed, horn-like appendages stand upright on either side of the central knot. A braid protrudes forward over the forehead. Slightly upturned slits pierce the eyes. A full, voluminous ruff of fine, black raffia fibers obscures the neck rings. Scarifications are indicated on the cheeks.

An empty medicine hole is present inside the dome of the mask. A small, tightly rolled piece of paper inscribed with Koranic text or magical Koranic symbols would have been inserted into the hole providing the wearer of the mask with protection against misfortune afforded by this concealed amulet.

Fig. 44

Fig. 45

HELMET MASK *(Sowei)*
Sherbro People: Sierra Leone
Materials: *Wood, pigment. H 16 in.*

In addition to being organized into two large lobes, the coiffure on this mask consists of two plaited braids emerging from the front and back that are tied to form an arch on top of the head. This arrangement is complemented by hanging, looped braids on either side of the head behind the ears. The sculpted form of the eyes resembles spectacles. The entire face is exceptionally low in the mask, appearing to push down and displace the neck rings.

Fig. 46

HELMET MASK (*Sowei*)
Vai People: Sierra Leone
Materials: *Wood, pigment, metal. H 16 in.*

This mask has a large, dome-shaped forehead, high-set ears, and thick neck rings. In contrast to the majority of *sowei* masks, the eyes are open apertures that are not adorned by lids, lashes, or scarifications. The coiffure composed of five high ridges is set off from the face by a narrow, carved band. An amulet is positioned on the central ridge. The edge of the central ridge is decorated by a slender band of silver-colored metal, and there is a disc of similar metal on top of the amulet. The ridged coiffure seen on this mask is an older hairstyle than the lobed coiffure. It is typically composed of an odd number of ridges with a central dominant ridge flanked by one or two smaller ridges.

Fig. 47

HELMET MASK (*Sowei*)
Sherbro People: Sierra Leone
Materials: *Wood, pigment.*
H 16 in.

A distinctive feature of this mask is a flat, box-shaped amulet situated on a thick central ridge flanked by two smaller ridges that form the coiffure. Bush cow horns that serve as additional amulets are carved on either side of the lateral hair ridges. The amulet is hollow, and it emits a faint rattling sound when the mask is shaken possibly due to "medicine" placed inside. A small repair is evident on the top of the amulet. There is no internal medicine hole. The forehead is set off by a carved arched strand of cowrie shells. The eyes are pierced by narrow, horizontal slits.

Fig. 48

HELMET MASK (*Sowei*)
Mende People: Sierra Leone
Materials: *Wood, pigment.*
H 15 in.

The tiered, pyramidal object on top of this mask is an amulet. It also duplicates the form of a type of cast brass goldweight. Complex braids and lobes define the coiffure. The ridge of the relatively long, slender nose rises above the eyes to insert high on the forehead to the level of the hairline. The eyes are pierced by slender, upwardly slanted slits. Five square medicine packets are carved in the form of a band around the back of the head and a small, empty medicine hole is present inside the dome of the mask.

Fig. 49

HELMET MASK (*Sowei*)
Sherbro People: Sierra Leone
Materials: *Wood, pigment.*
H 16 in.

The carved object that resembles an inverted table on top of this unusually conical mask **(Fig. 49)** is an amulet. Three tiers of additional amulets in the form of medicine bundles cover most of the coiffure around the head. These are typical of the various types of objects that were attached to women's hair for adornment as protection against evil or illness or to cure a headache. The eyes are pierced by horizontal slits.

HELMET MASK (*Sowei*)
Mende People: Sierra Leone
Materials: *Wood, pigment, mirror. H 17 in.*

A bifurcated topknot arises above the elaborate, plaited coiffure of this somewhat conical, finely finished mask **(Fig. 50)** with a round 1.75-inch mirror surrounded by delicate scrollwork in the front and back. The mirror has multiple roles in this context. It can see and repel the evil forces of witchcraft, thereby protecting the wearer of the mask. Mirrors also represent the surface of water, the border between land inhabited by people and the submerged world that is the domain of spirits who play a crucial role in the spiritual life of the *Bundu* Society.

Fig. 50

Fig. 51

HELMET MASK (*Sowei*)
Mende People: Sierra Leone
Materials: *Wood, pigment, coins. H 15.5 in.*

The number four appears to have had particular significance for the owner of this mask. Embedded in the surface of the ample forehead are four brass British coins picturing George VI, intended to indicate the high status of the wearer. The frontal part of the plaited coiffure is ornamented with strands of two types of medicine containers. One strand consists of four conical objects that represent the horns of the duiker antelope. Four rectangular amulets form the other strand. Four additional rectangular amulets are spread over the front, top, and back of a post on top of the head. One large horn-shaped amulet has been carved in the back of the head above the neck rings. The protective efficacy of amulets represented on a *sowei* mask was thought to be directly related to their number. Numerous amulets were also a sign of wealth because of the cost of having them carved. The plaited hair is gathered into two knobs on either side of the head, totaling four knobs. The wearer peered through narrow slits on either side of the chin. The eyes are intact.

HELMET MASK (*Sowei*)
Mende People: Sierra Leone
Materials: *Wood, pigment, metal. H 14.5 in.*

Fig. 52

The bird perched on the transverse ridge of this mask's coiffure rotates on a metal pin. This allows the bird to detect evil coming from any direction and to warn the wearer of the presence of a devil. Birds are perhaps the most honored of all animals among the Mende people and neighboring ethnic groups because they are perceived to have many traits in common with humans. They walk upright on their hind legs using their upper limbs (wings) for work (flying). A bird builds a home in which to raise offspring that is shared with a mate. They also communicate vocally and sing songs. The activities of birds are sometimes considered to be omens. Specially trained women are said to understand and interpret bird "speech" in order to foretell events. The hairstyle with a horizontal ridge is older than the style with ridges running from the front to the back of the head. The eyes of this mask are perforated by slender slits.

HELMET MASK (*Sowei*)
Mende People: Sierra Leone
Materials: *Wood, pigment, metal. H 14.5 in.*

A turtle sits atop the coiffure of this mask **(Fig. 53)** with a fine, polished surface. The turtle is credited with high intelligence because it carries its shell, a protective home, wherever it goes. As amphibious animals, turtles are believed to have the ability to communicate with spirits above and below the surface of water on behalf of people. The eyes of this mask are pierced by slightly upturned slits. Three-quarter inch in diameter brass wire earrings are present in the ear lobes.

Fig. 53

Fig. 54

HELMET MASK (*Sowei*)
Temne People: Sierra Leone
Materials: *Wood, pigment.*
H 17.5 in.

The coiffure of this mask **(Fig. 54)** consists of layers of braids swirling counter clockwise around a central, ring-necked post that supports a small female head. The face of the mask is relatively large, occupying about half of the front, and it is carved in a naturalistic manner except for exceptionally small ears. The eyes are pierced by horizontal slits beneath overhanging upper lids. There is an oval viewing hole on either side of the chin.

Fig. 55

HELMET MASK (Sowei)
Bassa People: Liberia
Materials: *Wood, pigment. H 13.5 in.*

Many Bassa *sowei* masks **(Fig. 56)** do not have prominent neck rings that typify Mende masks of this type. The small face, open eye apertures, and white pigment dots applied to the forehead are characteristic features of a Bassa *sowei* mask. In this instance, the hair is braided over the back and sides of the head and in an arch over the face. The front of the coiffure consists of four horn-shaped objects that may represent amulets.

Fig. 56

HELMET MASK (Sowei)
Temne People: Sierra Leone
Materials: *Wood, pigment. H 17.5 in.*

Layered braids are distributed in an asymmetric, swirling, counter clockwise arrangement on this mask **(Fig. 55)**. A hanging, looped braid is present on either side of the head. The large face with naturalistic features, except for very small ears, occupies about half of the front of the mask. Three snakes writhing around the head of the mask are probably a reference to Mami Wata, a water spirit who is often represented with snakes. Cross-shaped scarifications are present on the cheeks. The eyes are pierced by narrow, upturned slits, and there are oval viewing holes on either side of the chin.

Fig. 57

HELMET MASK (*Sowei*)
Mende People: Sierra Leone
Materials: *Wood, pigment.*
H 15 in.

The *gonde* mask is worn by a woman dressed in a ragged costume of cloth or raffia who begs for money from the audience and acts as a clown offering comic relief. She is a parody of the beauty and dignity represented by the *sowei* mask. By highlighting the ugliness that results from failure to maintain proper grooming and comportment, *gonde* reinforces the power of the beauty prized by the *Sande* Society and its initiates. The *gonde* mask is usually an old, somewhat deteriorated *sowei* mask that is decorated with kaolin or white paint.

In this example, white paint denotes scarifications on the cheeks and outer corners of the eyes. A white dot has been placed between eyebrows painted white. There is also white paint on the upper lip and upper eyelids. A faint trace of red paint is present on the vermilion borders of the lips. The eyes are pierced by narrow, upturned slits. The coiffure consists of four lobes that are gathered to form a knot on top of the head. A scroll-shaped amulet hangs from a strap on the back of the head.

FACE MASKS (*Gongoli*)
Mende People: Sierra Leone
Materials: *Wood, pigment, metal.* Fig. 58: *H 27 in.*; Fig. 59: *H 23 in.*; Fig. 60: *H 16 in.*

The *gongoli* masquerade is found among the Mende and neighboring people, including the Vai, Sherbro, Gola, and Temne. Its performances are intended to entertain. *Gongoli* is danced by a man who wears a disheveled raffia costume. He is accompanied by a group of rowdy boys and men who sing while banging sticks on bottles and cans. *Gongoli* acts as a clown who satirizes the townspeople and claims the ability to perform magical tricks. He begs for money and rice. Because of the way he dresses and behaves, *Gongoli* is the antithesis of the composed beauty of the *sowei* mask. His antics are intended to reduce tension at solemn events, such as funerals, by providing comic relief.

In contrast to *sowei* masks that have a relatively stereotypical appearance, J.V.O. Richards has noted that *gongoli* masks are carved in many forms. Each of the three Mende *gongoli* masks illustrated here has intentionally ugly masculine facial features consisting of protruding ears, a big, open mouth, and a large, prominent nose. The eyes and mouth of the oldest and most abstract mask are roughly carved squares **(Fig. 58)**. Only one of several metal teeth remains. The 23-inch tall mask of intermediate age has a knob-like beard, large ears, a gaping, asymmetrical mouth, and white, painted, cross-hatch designs on its cheeks, possibly representing scarifications **(Fig. 59)**. A hole in the top of the 16-inch tall mask **(Fig. 60)** may have held something that mimicked the type of sculpted object found on top of a *sowei* mask.

Fig. 58

Fig. 59

Fig. 60

Fig. 61

Fig. 62

HELMET MASKS *(Gongoli)*
Temne People: Sierra Leone
Materials: *Wood, pigment.*
Fig. 61: *H 17 in.*; Fig. 62: *24 in.*

The two *gongoli* masks attributed to the Temne people illustrated here have unattractive facial features with a more overtly masculine appearance than those of the Mende *gongoli*. The smaller mask has a bald head and a beard. A substantial piece of hand woven cloth that covered the head of the masker remains attached to the back **(Fig. 61)**. The helmet-shaped mask **(Fig. 62)** exhibits an odd combination of neck rings reminiscent of a *sowei* mask, an open mouth with one remaining tooth, and two large, bovine horns.

HELMET MASK *(Ya Ma Ma Coni Coni)*
Sherbro People: Sierra Leone
Materials: *Wood, pigment, mirror. H 9 in.*

The name of this mask means "the cunning mask" (Jeremiah Cole, personal communication, 2011). The entranced dancer, covered by an outfit of raffia, cloth, and fur, whirls around wielding a knife. The mirrors help the dancer detect witches and liars as well as deflect the spell of witchcraft in the form of the "evil eye." The mask is decorated with carvings of animal horns that replicate containers for magical substances and protective amulets made from antelope or goat horns.

This mask, sculpted in wood, duplicates similar traditional headpieces built around a bamboo frame that is covered with red, white, and black cloth, fur, cowrie shells, amulets, and mirrors. The mirror on the top, as well as mirrors around the perimeter, and the red, white, and black paint are essential features of this mask.

Masks of this type are worn by *gbini* and *goboi* maskers who can be distinguished by their costumes and their performances. *Gbini*, representing the power of the senior chief, appears at events involving the high chief and his family. His costume includes a leopard skin that symbolizes the chief's authority. *Goboi* who wears monkey skin is less powerful than *gbini*. It is associated with secondary chiefs and appears more frequently than *gbini*. The mask illustrated here is said to be a *goboi* mask (Jeremiah Cole, personal communication, 2011).

Fig. 63

Fig. 64

FOREHEAD MASK (*Geh-Naw*)
Bassa People: Liberia
Materials: *Wood, pigment.*
H 9 in.

This mask represents a non-human spirit of the *Nor* Society. It is worn on the forehead attached to a woven basketry framework. The coiffure of the mask consists of hair knots and braids. The masquerade performs with gliding movements to entertain the audience at various celebrations.

The Ode-Lay and Jolly Society Masquerades in Freetown, Sierra Leone

The earliest British settlement in Sierra Leone dates from 1787, when about 350 poor black people were brought from London. The population increased in 1792 with the arrival in Freetown of about 1000 Nova Scotia ex-slaves, black Loyalists who had fought with the British during the American Revolution. More than 500 Jamaican Maroons were transported to Freetown in 1800. In the succeeding decades, following the abolition of slavery by Britain in the early nineteenth century, Freetown became the site for the liberation of many thousands of Africans found aboard slave ships captured by the British navy. Many of the freed Nupe, Ibo, Ibibio, Igbo, and Yoruba slaves, who originated in Nigeria, revived their religious traditions in Sierra Leone. The most influential Yoruba secret societies included the following: Egungun, dedicated to the worship of ancestors; Hunting, dedicated to Ogun, the god of iron and fire, associated with hunting and war; Shango, dedicated to the god of thunder; and Gelede, dedicated to maintaining prosperity and celebrating the role of women.

Masquerades organized by these societies, drawing upon forms remembered from Nigeria, appeared by the 1830s as parades in which members displayed their idols or "devils" to the accompaniment of dance and music, especially drumming. These processions became rallying points for the societies, serving to promote the health, welfare, and success of their members. Hunting Societies carried their "devils" in masquerades before and after a hunt or to honor a dead member. Masquerade processions of Gelede, Egungun, Shango, and other Societies were dedicated to curing illness, maintaining the health and prosperity of society members, and relationships with ancestors.

Illness was attributed to witchcraft that could be confronted through the application and display of "medicines." In Nigeria, goats and sheep had been sacrificed as part of masquerades to cure illness, and the heads of sacrificed animals became medicine when worn on the heads of masqueraders. In Sierra Leone, these animal heads were replaced by carved wooden replicas. Over the succeeding decades, the Yoruba-based masquerade societies evolved in response to various influences including the rise of a Creole middle class, exposure to Western, Islamic, Hindu, and Oriental culture, and styles introduced by other immigrants as well as economic growth during and after the World Wars.

The influx into Freetown of new immigrants from the countryside, especially after World War II, led to the formation of numerous Ode-Lay and Jolly (pronounced like the French word, "joli") Societies composed largely of unemployed, uneducated young men who were not eligible to become members of the traditional societies because of their low economic status. Cloth, an important aesthetic and prestige commodity became a fundamental component of Ode-Lay and Jolly Society masquerades. The costumes and masks created for Ode-lay and Jolly Society masquerades were inspired by the fancy aesthetic of Gelede and Egungun Society masquerades and the fierce aesthetic of the Hunting Societies. These masquerades were performed at Christmas time, Boxing Day, and New Years Day as well as at other celebrations.

In contrast to Ode-Lay Societies that were organized by descendants of the Yoruba, Igbo, and other predominantly Nigerian ethnic groups, Jolly Societies that arose in the same era were dominated by Temne people who were native to the Sierra Leone countryside. Nonetheless, Jolly Society masquerades derived their aesthetics from sources similar to those that gave rise to Ode-Lay Society masquerades. Fierce elements are typically absent from Jolly Society masquerades, whereas Ode-Lay Society masquerades often combine fancy and fierce aesthetics. Fancy refers to the use of brightly colored cloth, lace, Christmas tree ornaments, beads, feathers, trinkets of various sorts, mirrors, and sparkling objects such as aluminum foil. The headdress of a fancy costume may be constructed around a wire or wood board armature or it may consist of a wooden carving attached to an armature. In the context of the Ode-Lay Society masquerade, fierce is interpreted as meaning powerful and frightening as well as visually striking. The fierce aesthetic is expressed in a carved headpiece, or *erie*, representing the head of a leopard, antelope, goat, sheep, or a composite head with elements of two or more of the foregoing animals. Various medicine objects are attached to the vest-like cloak, or *hampa*, that covers the torso of the "devil" including porcupine quills embedded in small gourds, bullet casings, animal skins, snail shells dipped in poisons, and antelope horns filled with medicine powder. Sometimes, wooden replicas of gourds with porcupine quills appear as part of a masquerade headpiece. John Nunley, the foremost expert on Ode-Lay and Jolly Society masquerades, has noted that "the quills are likened to endless rounds of bullets, they just keep coming, and as well like showers of arrows." Horns protruding from the headpiece are thought to have the capacity to mediate between man and the world of spirits. The horns transmit messages from the spirits that inform man of his destiny. The emblems of fierceness are intended protect against the malevolent effects of witchcraft.

Various aspects of Mami Wata (Pidgen English for "mother of water"), a seductive, and dangerous female water spirit of foreign origin, are represented in Ode-Lay and Jolly Society masquerade headpieces. Venerated in much of Africa, especially in countries bordering on the African Atlantic, and the Atlantic rim of the Americas affected by the African diaspora, she promotes fertility, wealth, and abundance. Important features of Mami Wata are her association with water and with snakes. She is a jealous spirit who demands that her followers be faithful to her at the of risk dire consequences. Painted images and sculptures of Mami Wata appear to derive from several sources. One is the European image of the seductive siren or mermaid with a fishtail who rises from the water that appeared as a figurehead on some of the European ships that transported luxury goods to West African ports. Some representations of Mami Wata have wings that may be derived from images widely circulated in Muslim communities of al-Buraq, the mythical winged half-horse, half-human, Centaur-like creature that carried the prophet Mohamed to heaven. Involvement of snakes in Mami Wata reflects the long-standing association of snakes with water spirits in West Africa. In addition, recent investigations have traced a connection between Mami Wata and a European printed portrait of an exotic circus snake charmer with a snake draped over her shoulders. This image was reproduced in India where motifs related to Hindu gods and goddesses were introduced before the picture was widely distributed in West Africa.

Hindu people from the Indian sub-continent have been major retailers and shopkeepers in Sierra Leone since the nineteenth century, selling a variety of goods including photolithographs of Hindu deities that may have inspired aspects of many of the Temne head crest sculptures illustrated in this book. Representations of Mami Wata often display the Hindu forehead dot *(bindi)* that protects against the "evil eye" and other decorative motifs of Hindu origin such as a forehead pendant and curls hanging on the side of the head. *Bindi* means a "drop or dot." It is traditionally a spot of red pigment applied low on the center of the forehead between the eyebrows. This position is considered to be the locus of hidden wisdom, concentration, and the site of the "third eye." The *bindi* protects against evil spirits and bad luck.

Most of the Temne helmet and head crest masks illustrated and described in this volume have smooth surfaces on which the effects of the passage of years are clearly evident in the form of discolored paint, layered paint, wear and tear, and oxidation of unpainted wood. These masks were most likely made for use in traditional masquerades. A small number of the head crest masks that we describe as "recently carved" have relatively rough surfaces covered with a single layer of bright, fresh paint, and exposed wood with minimal evidence of oxidation. The latter new sculptures may have been made for traditional use or for export and sale on the art market.

HELMET MASKS
Temne Or Lokko People: Sierra Leone
Materials: *Wood, paint, metal.* Fig. 65: H 23.5 in.; Fig. 66: H 27 in.

These exceptional Jolly Society masks honor Mami Wata, a powerful water spirit. Each consists of a female figure with articulated arms seated astride a *sowei*-style helmet mask with four faces. The multiple faces look in the four cardinal directions to detect witchcraft. They recall the vigilance needed in the nineteenth century to avoid capture as a slave and the danger presented by Mende warriors or Kamajors and rebel military groups such as the Revolutionary United Front (RUF) during the Sierra Leone civil war in the past two decades. The moveable arms of the female figures may be a reference to Temne twin sculptures that have similarly articulated arms.

The arms of the brown figure are shown upraised from the articulated shoulders **(Fig. 65)**. Flexed at the elbows and articulated at the shoulders, the arms of the white figure are positioned facing forward **(Fig. 66)**. The masks have Hindu-inspired, painted, decorative motifs that are associated with Mami Wata. The wearer was able to see through small apertures in the neck. The triangular objects between the faces on the mask with a white figure **(Fig. 66)** may be protective amulets inspired by the Kaballah magical triangle known as "abra kadabra."

Fig. 65

Fig. 66

Fig. 67

Fig. 68

HELMET MASK
Temne Or Lokko People: Sierra Leone
Materials: *Wood, paint, metal.*
H 22.5 in.

This unusual Jolly Society helmet mask consists of a female figure with arms articulated at the shoulders seated astride a helmet-like base consisting of four faces whose chins serve as supporting legs. The reverse-S designs on the female figure's chest may represent snakes. The distinctive structure of the mask raises the possibility that it might have been used as a shrine to Mami Wata. The female figures on this and the preceding two masks are very similar and most likely are the work of the same artist. Seen in profile, the three female figures on these masks have features reminiscent of sculptures made by the Baga people in Guinea to whom the Temne are linguistically and culturally related.

Fig. 69

Fig. 70

HELMET MASK
Temne Or Lokko People:
Sierra Leone
Materials: *Wood, paint. H 18 in.*

The helmet component of this mask is similar to those of the previously described **(Figs. 65-68)** *Mami Wata*-associated masks in that it has four faces with Hindu-inspired features. However, the figure on the top is a man who leans forward to support himself on his hands in a quadruped, acrobatic stance. He is most likely one of the acrobats who entertain during a Jolly Society masquerade. In Sierra Leone sculpture, the presence of a man above a female refers to the power of women, giving rise to the commonly used expression, "woman tote man." This mask has sculptural features in common with the previously illustrated Mami Wata helmet masks and might be the work of the same carver.

HELMET MASK
Temne People: Sierra Leone
Materials: *Wood, paint. H 17.5 in.*

The male figure in military garb is probably a member of the Revolutionary United Front (RUF) holding an AK47 machine gun that might have been bought with blood diamonds. He is seated astride a Janus-faced shallow helmet mask. As is evident in the side view **(Fig. 72)**, the eyes of the face on the front of the helmet are open, possibly symbolizing life, whereas those of the rear face are closed suggesting death. The mask celebrates military power and reveals in graphic terms the severe impact that the war had on Sierra Leone. This mask could have been used in either an Ode-Lay or a Jolly Society masquerade.

Fig. 71

Fig. 72

HELMET MASK
Temne People: Sierra Leone
Materials: *Wood, paint. H 14 in.*

This Janus mask has the face of a bearded man with open eyes on one side and a female face with full neck rings, open eyes, and cheek scarifications on the other side. Straddling the top of the mask from side to side is a female figure seated in a palanquin that is carried by two porters who are reminiscent of domestic slavery in former days. In addition to supporting the litter, one man holds a horn to his mouth to announce the arrival of an important woman. The style of this mask is similar to that of the mask in **(Figs. 71, 72)** and is probably the work of the same sculptor.

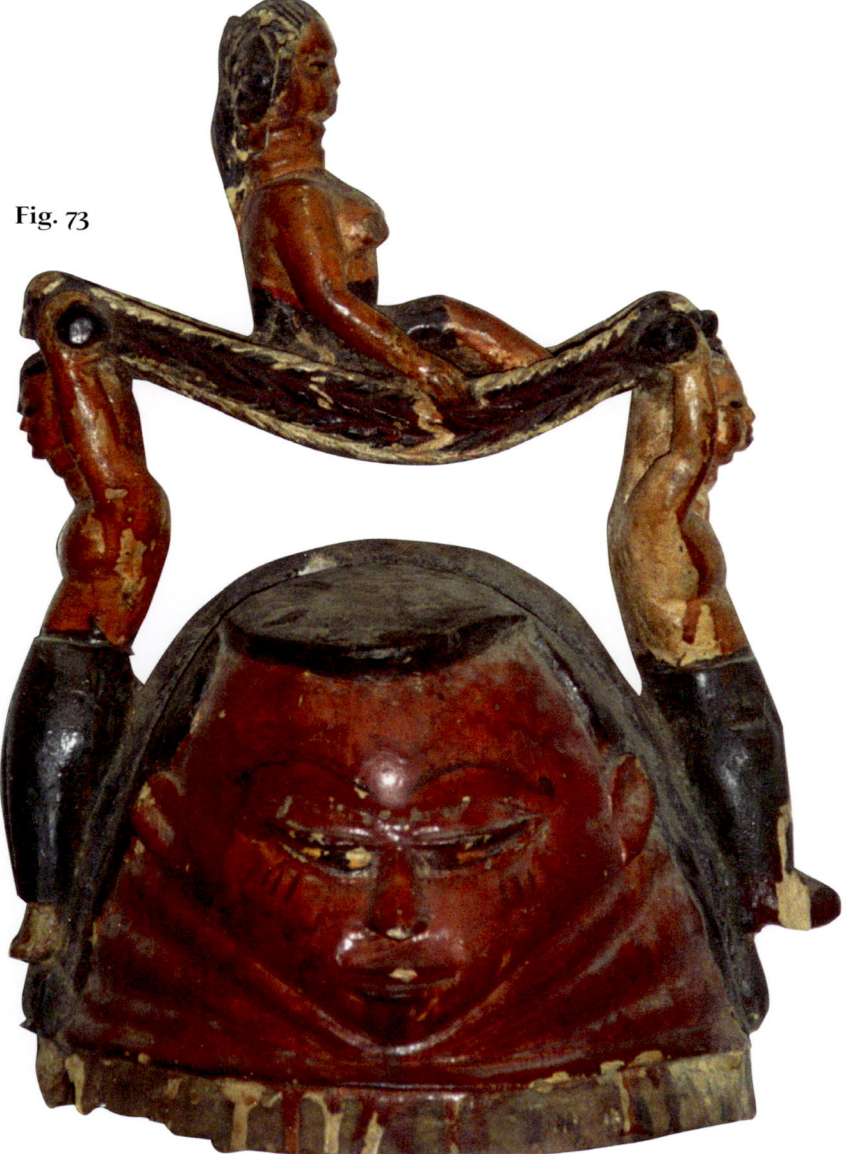

Fig. 74

Fig. 73

HEAD CREST MASKS
Temne People: Sierra Leone
Materials: *Wood, paint, beads, cloth.*
Fig. 75: *H 10.5 in.*; Fig. 76: *H 14.5 in.*;
Fig. 77: *H 17 in.*; Fig. 78: *H 18 in.*;
Fig. 79: *H 12.5 in.*

Illustrated here are four female and one male bust head crest masks. Each is painted with a different bright enamel color and has a distinctive coiffure. The surfaces of three female busts are decorated with spots or patches of color that contrast with the underlying base color **(Figs. 75, 77, 78)**. Wooden beads are attached to the crown of the head of the 14.5-inch tall female bust **(Fig. 76)**. In contrast to *sowei* helmet masks, the facial features are realistically sculpted in proper proportion. The female busts have neck rings whereas the neck of the male bust is covered by cloth tied as a jaunty scarf **(Fig. 79)**. Colorful scarves are often used as part of a Jolly Society masquerade costume and may be incorporated into masks as well **(Fig. 118)**.

Fig. 75

Fig. 76

Fig. 77

Fig. 78

Fig. 79

65

Fig. 80

Fig. 81

Fig. 82

HEAD CREST MASKS
Temne People: Sierra Leone
Materials: *Wood, paint, cloth, nails, decorative material.* Figs. 80, 81: *H 23 in.*; Fig. 82: *H 18.5 in.*

Depicted here are two arresting head crest masks in the form of female and male busts. The style of the sculptures and identical way they are painted indicate that they are the work of the same artist. The bosom of the female figure has been created with foam rubber to mimic a padded bra **(Figs. 80, 81)**. Her chest and abdomen are clothed in a dress, and her arms are articulated at the shoulders. The male bust consists only of a head and ringed neck **(Fig. 82)**. The acutely angled coiffure of the male bust may represent a jaunty knit cap. These figures probably appeared in Jolly Society masquerades.

Fig. 83

HEAD CREST MASK
Temne People: Sierra Leone
Materials: *Wood, paint, yarn, Christmas ornament, decorative material. H 21 in.*

This female head crest bust represents Mami Wata. Two snakes encircle her neck and rise behind her to appear over her head. Her hair has been fashioned from cotton yarn, and a glass Christmas ornament hangs like an earring from one ear. The use of non-indigenous decorative material such as yarn, tinsel, mirrors, and various ornaments is common in Temne Jolly Society head crest sculptures.

Fig. 84

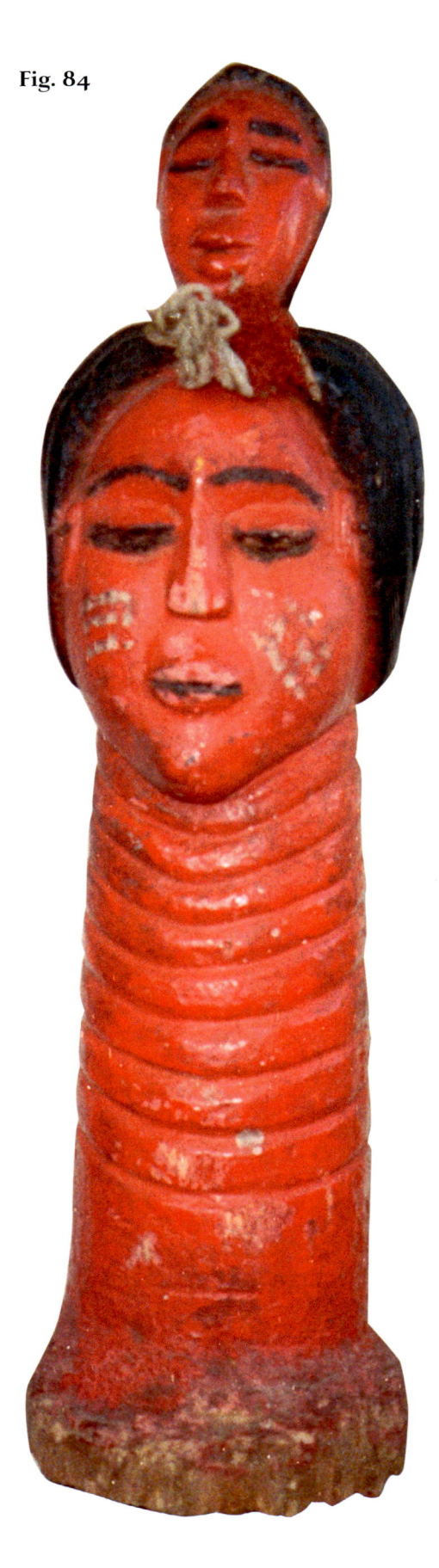

HEAD CREST MASK
Temne People: Sierra Leone
Materials: *Wood, paint, coconut shell, metal, yarn. H 27 in.*

This Jolly Society female bust head crest mask is distinguished by an exceptionally tall, ringed neck. The base of this old, repainted sculpture is substantially eroded, and it has been placed on the shell of a coconut to which it is attached by a nail driven from below through a small hole in the coconut. As a result, the sculpture can rotate freely on the coconut shell. This head crest probably appeared in a Jolly masquerade. The second, small head above the female bust is probably that of a man, representing men's dependence on women that is crystallized in the expression, "woman tote man" **(see Figs. 69,70)**.

Fig. 85

HEAD CREST MASK
Temne People: Sierra Leone
Materials: *Wood, paint, yarn, decorative material. H 20.5 in.*

The larger, Janus-faced female head of this mask has similar faces in the front and back whereas the smaller female head situated on top has a single, frontal face. The braided hair of the upper female head is drawn together in a central bun. The Janus head is adorned with yarn and other decorative material. We believe that this head crest mask appeared in a Jolly Society masquerade.

Fig. 86

HEAD CREST MASK
Temne People: Sierra Leone
Materials: *Wood, paint, nails.*
H 26.5 in.

A deer head with antlers resembling an elk rises above the female bust at the base of this Ode-Lay Hunters' Society head crest mask. Recently, it has been reported that the stuffed heads of dead elk have been attached to Ode-Lay Society head crests. In her book, *Maske*, Phyllis Galembo illustrated two Temne Jolly masquerades with deer heads, one of which was carved and the other was an embalmed real head. She reported that deer heads were "once made of papier mache or carved in wood ... (but) ...some have now been replaced by actual animal heads preserved by taxidermy and sent to Freetown by expatriates living in the United States."

In this instance, the woman's neck rings have been painted rather than sculpted. Nails hammered into the unpainted base of this and many other Temne head crest masks were used for attaching an armature of wire or wood that supported the sculpture and for suspending a costume with attached decorative material including amulets.

HEAD CREST MASK
Temne People: Sierra Leone
Materials: *Wood, paint, nails. H 26.5 in.*

The realistically sculpted female head of this Ode-Lay Society head crest bust is Janus-faced. Hindu-inspired motifs were used to decorate both faces, including a red forehead dot. The necklaces with cowrie shells in the front and back are sculpted as are decorative elements of the coiffures associated with the two faces. The fierce leopard head peering forward through intent, feline eyes with its mouth opened to expose menacing fangs, contrasts sharply with the beautiful, fancy aesthetic of the female bust. This effect is enhanced by the miniature versions of similar fierce, fanged leopard heads sculpted on either side of the bust in place of the arms. The object protruding from the back of the large fierce head consists of a bundle of slender, red, wooden objects that resemble hot peppers or flames encased in a wire coil that is wrapped in cloth. It serves as a power instrument intended to reinforce the animal's dangerous aura as well as a protective amulet. This bust head crest exemplifies the fierce and fancy aesthetic of an Ode-Lay masquerade, referencing the Leopard Society that played an active role in the slave trade in Sierra Leone. Cowrie shells that appear in the necklaces and other ornaments were one of the forms of currency used in the buying and selling of slaves.

Fig. 87

Fig. 88

HEAD CREST MASK
Temne People: Sierra Leone
Materials: *Wood, paint, nails, porcupine quills. H 15.5 in.*

This relatively symmetrical Janus Ode-Lay Society head crest displays two fierce animal heads painted with different colors. The shape of the wooden base is reminiscent of the basketry base found on Nigerian Ejagham head crests. Although not specific, the heads have features suggestive of goats and leopards. The open mouth with exposed teeth and lolling tongue is found on many fierce Ode-Lay animal heads. In this instance, the ferocity of the sculpture is enhanced by porcupine quills inserted into holes in round objects that are sculpted representations of small calabashes. The quills are a form of defense that serves as a reminder of nineteenth century Temne warriors who covered themselves with metal spikes as protection against capture by slave traders.

Fig. 89

Fig. 90

Fig. 91

HEAD CREST MASK
Temne People: Sierra Leone
Materials: *Wood, paint, nails. H 29 in. (without horns)*

The base of this Ode-Lay Society head crest has three female faces, respectively, on the front and on either side. Arching forward above the base is the bust of a fierce, composite animal with a ringed neck, prominent ears, and an open mouth. Two S-shaped, detachable horns with painted striations that represent the rings on an antelope's horns are fitted into sockets in the top of the animal head. The animal's large, beak-like nose and open, round, staring eyes are evident in the frontal view. The features of the sculpted animal suggest the body of a snake with the head of a goat and the horns of an antelope.

73

HEAD CREST MASK
Temne People: Sierra Leone
Materials: *Wood, paint, nails. H 20 in. (without horns)*

The lower half of this Ode-Lay Society head crest mask consists of a fancy female bust with Hindu-inspired carved and painted facial features and prominent neck rings. Detachable, painted wings have been inserted into sockets on the top of her head. A composite, spotted, fierce animal head with an open mouth, lolling tongue, and neck rings rises from the center of the woman's head. Curved, antelope-style, detachable horns painted to match the wings have been inserted into sockets on top of the animal's head. As is typical of most two-tiered, Temne Ode-Lay head crests, the head of the fierce animal on top is smaller than that of the lower female bust. Whatever their symbolic significance, these proportions add to the artistic appeal of the sculpture and help the wearer to keep it balanced on his head.

Fig. 92

Fig. 93

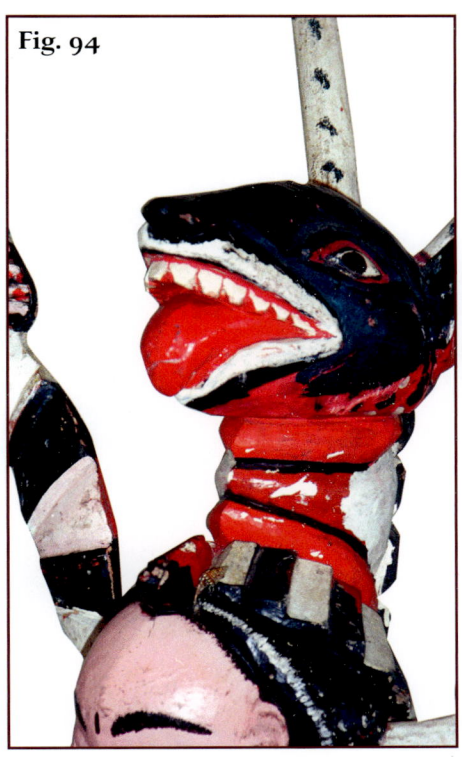

Fig. 94

HEAD CREST MASK
Temne People: Sierra Leone
Materials: *Wood, paint, nails.*
H 42.5 in. (with horns)

This brightly painted, recently carved Ode-Lay Society head crest features a fancy female bust whose face has a Hindu-inspired forehead dot. Carved light and dark rectangular objects around the woman's head are amulets. Sockets on either side of the back of the woman's head hold blunt wings that have been painted with a striped design. Vertical horns painted to match the wings have been inserted into the fierce leopard head. The leopard has an open mouth that displays white teeth and a lolling tongue.

Fig. 95

HEAD CREST MASK
Temne People: Sierra Leone
Materials: *Wood, paint, nails. H 22 in.*

A snake encircles the ringed neck of the fierce leopard head at the top of this Ode-Lay Society head crest mask. The bust below is Janus-faced with slightly different female faces having Hindu-inspired features in front and back. The coiffure is braided with dependant braids on either side of the frontal face. A hair knot containing a jewel protrudes above the forehead. Two well-carved, detachable wings are present. Horns are absent.

Fig. 96

HEAD CREST MASK
Temne People: Sierra Leone
Materials: *Wood, paint, nails. H 22 in.*

The Janus-headed lower portion of this Ode-Lay Society mask has a female head with parallel braids and a spotted animal head representing a leopard in back. A composite, spotted fierce animal head with an open mouth and protruding tongue peers over the top of the human head. There are no apertures for wings or horns. The forms of the human and fierce animal heads are similar to those in the previous mask **(Figs. 95, 96)** suggesting that they are the work of the same carver.

Fig. 97

Fig. 98

Fig. 99

Fig. 100

HEAD CREST MASK
Temne People: Sierra Leone
Materials: *Wood, paint, nails, metal, porcupine quills. H 30 in. (without horns)*

The horns, wings and fish tail of this brightly painted Ode-Lay Society head crest mask are detachable **(Fig. 98)**. The hair is braided with dependant, hinged braids that swing back and forth on both sides of the face. Oval objects painted on the surfaces of the wings represent cowrie shells used as currency that are a sign of wealth. The forked tail is a reference to the water spirit, Mami Wata **(Fig. 99)**. Protruding from the back of the bust is a wooden ball with many holes into which porcupine quills were placed to enhance the ferocity of the assemblage **(Fig. 100)**. The spotted leopard's head sports curved horns with forked ends that mirror the shape of the tail. The leopard head is hinged and capable of swinging about 10 degrees forward and backward. The nails and metal ring around the base were used to attach the costume.

Fig. 101

HEAD CREST MASK
Temne People: Sierra Leone
Materials: *Wood, paint. H 35 in.*

Together the kneeling female figures on the upper part of this recently carved Ode-Lay society head crest sculpture hold the shaft of a pounder used to prepare grain in one hand and a tray for winnowing the grain to remove the chaff after it has been pounded in the other. The sculptor has used the braided hair of the female bust in a very imaginative way to support the female figures. The female bust has Hindu-inspired decorative features that are a reference to the water spirit, Mami Wata.

79

Fig. 102

Fig. 103

HEAD CREST MASK
Temne People: Sierra Leone
Materials: *Wood, paint. H 28 in.*

The upper portion of this Ode-Lay Society head crest mask with a Janus-faced base displays an interesting combination of figures. Flanking the central, fierce leopard head with an open mouth exposing ferocious, white teeth, are two kneeling female figures holding the heads of snakes above their heads. The female figures and the Janus female bust that forms the base have Hindu-inspired features that in combination with the presence of snakes are a reference to the water spirit, Mami Wata.

Fig. 104

HEAD CREST MASK
Temne People: Sierra Leone
Materials: *Wood, paint. H 32 in.*

This extraordinary three-tiered Ode-Lay Society sculpture, recently carved from a single block of wood, displays a female figure kneeling on the back of fierce bird that is struggling with five snakes. The bird has managed to grasp one snake in its powerful, golden beak. Two snakes are biting the sides of the bird's neck and another pair of snakes is biting the bird's wings. The woman's fingers are curled around empty sockets. The Hindu-inspired decorative motifs on the female figure seated on the bird and the female bust, combined with the multiple snakes, are a reference to the water spirit, Mami Wata.

HEAD CREST MASK
Temne People: Sierra Leone
Materials: *Wood, paint. H 25 in.*

This fanciful Jolly Society sculpture, recently carved from a single block of wood, displays a seated female figure with Hindu-inspired features wearing a leopard skin that covers one breast. With one hand she is holding a radio or a cell phone to an ear. Two pairs of detachable wings are inserted in sockets in the head of the lower female bust. A third pair of wings supported by arched snakes arises from the base. The bust has elaborate, Hindu-inspired features painted on the face and carved in the coiffure. Her face is set off by a brightly colored, carved, jeweled crown.

Fig. 105

HEAD CREST MASK
Temne People: Sierra Leone
Materials: *Wood, paint. H 31 in.*

The upper part of this recently carved Ode-Lay Society head crest mask consists of a female figure, painted brown, who is seated on the back and head of a ferocious crocodile. In each of her hands, the woman is holding a fish by its tail. She is decorated with bracelets around the upper parts of her arms and legs as well as straps crossing on her chest. The lower part of the head crest is a female bust with Hindu-inspired decorative motifs painted on the face and in the carved coiffure. Veined wings have been inserted in sockets in the back of the head of the female bust.

Fig. 106

Fig. 107

Fig. 108

HEAD CREST MASK
Temne People: Sierra Leone
Materials: *Wood, paint, nails.*
H 29.5 in.

The upper, kneeling female figure holding two snakes in this recently carved Jolly Society head crest mask and the lower female bust both display painted and carved Hindu-inspired motifs. In this context, the upper figure may represent the water spirit, Mami Wata. Cowrie shells incorporated into the coiffure of the bust and jewelry of the upper figure are a reference to wealth and the power that wealth brings. During the period of the slave trade, the cost of a slave or a bride was 20,000 cowries, an amount referred to in some quarters as "captif."

HEAD CREST MASK
Temne People: Sierra Leone
Materials: *Wood, paint. H 28 in.*

Fig. 109

This unusual Ode-Lay Society head crest mask **(Fig. 109)** depicts a man with sporty attire and coiffure seated on a ferocious lion with bared teeth. The man holds a sword in his right hand. The lion stands astride a prone female figure whose head juts forward between the lion's front legs in a manner similar to that of a sculptural figurehead at the bow of a European sailing ship or the depiction of Al-Buraq, the mythical, Centaur-like, winged horse with a human head that carried the Prophet Mohammed to heaven. Lions appear prominently in the Sierra Leone coat of arms.

Fig. 110

FACE MASK
Temne People: Sierra Leone
Materials: *Wood, paint, nails. H 9 in.*

This Jolly masquerade face mask **(Fig. 110)** shows extensive wear with abrasion of the brightly painted surface. A single, deeply carved scarification is present on each cheek. The central lobe of the coiffure contains a conical hole with the wide end at the top. It has been suggested that this hole contained a receptacle for "medicine." The colors used to paint this mask and the facial features resemble those of a mask created by Abdul Aziz Lasisi Alayode Mukhtarr (Ajani) illustrated in plate 5 by John W. Nunley in his book, *Moving with the Face of the Devil*.

FACE MASK
Temne People: Sierra Leone
Materials: Wood, paint. H 9 in.

This blue, male Jolly Society face mask **(Fig. 112)** with narrow eye slits and parted coiffure has eyebrows, eyelashes, and cheek scarifications indicated with yellow paint. The style of the carving and painted details is similar to that of **(Fig. 111)**, suggesting they may be the work of a single artist, possibly Abdul Aziz Lasisi Alayode Mukhtarr, who was active making similar masks in the latter part of the 20th century.

Fig. 111

Fig. 112

FACE MASK
Temne People: Sierra Leone
Materials: Wood, paint. H 10 in.

This female Jolly Society face mask **(Fig. 111)** with an orange face has a lobed hairstyle and narrow, slit eye apertures. Lashes are indicated by lines painted along the edges of the eyelids.

FACE MASKS
Lokko People: Sierra Leone
Materials: *Wood, paint.* Fig. 113: *H 11 in.;* Fig. 114: *H 6.5 in.*

The rounded contours, small ears and mouths, and the looped hairlines of these two masks are similar. The facial surfaces of both masks exhibit considerable wear. The larger yellow male mask was carved from dense, relatively heavy wood **(Fig. 113)**, whereas the small, green female mask was carved from lightweight, fragile wood **(Fig. 114)**. They were used in Jolly Society masquerades. Similar masks appear in pairs in masquerades of "fancy" dress societies in Ivory Coast and Ghana, supporting the concept of a regional archetype that resulted from early trade patterns in the area.

Fig. 113

Fig. 114

Fig. 115

Fig. 116

FACE MASK
Temne People: Sierra Leone
Materials: *Wood, paint, cloth, synthetic hair, decorative objects.*
H 13.5 in.

This female Jolly Society mask with a brown face, slit eye apertures, and smiling mouth has a coiffure of abundant black synthetic hair that is embellished with various decorative objects including beads, jewelry, ribbons, and a mirror as protection against evil spirits. A small wooden antelope head is affixed to the hair above the forehead. Hanging from the mask is a black cotton print cloth with a brightly colored flower border. The forehead dot is a Hindu-inspired motif.

Fig. 117

FACE MASK
Temne People: Sierra Leone
Materials: *Wood, paint, wire, yarn, decorative objects. H 21 in.*

This bi-level female mask was probably used in a Jolly Society masquerade. The lower portion is a face mask with up-curving slit eyes. Attached on top is a small, three-dimensional, female head with neck rings and a smiling countenance. The mask and upper head are decorated with ruffs formed from strands of white yarn, and both have hair fashioned from synthetic fibers. At an earlier time, the ruffs were made of fur or were boas created from ostrich and down feathers that were extremely valuable commodities in the slave trade. A round mirror providing protection against evil spirits has been suspended from coiffure of the mask and a cloth shroud that would have disguised the wearer hangs from the back of the mask. In performance, the mirror sparkled with reflected light and the articulated upper head rocked back and forth.

89

FACE MASK
Temne People: Sierra Leone
Materials: *Wood, paint, wire, cloth. H 29 in.*

This elaborately constructed Jolly Society mask consists of two pink face masks with upward-turned slit eye apertures that are connected by multiple strands of wire. The ends of many wire strands are bent to create leaf-like loops representing amulets that have been wrapped with thin cloth of the type found in a silk designer scarf. In performance, the upper face and the various cloth-covered wire extensions were set in motion. Sierra Leone artists who create masks such as this are called "wire benders."

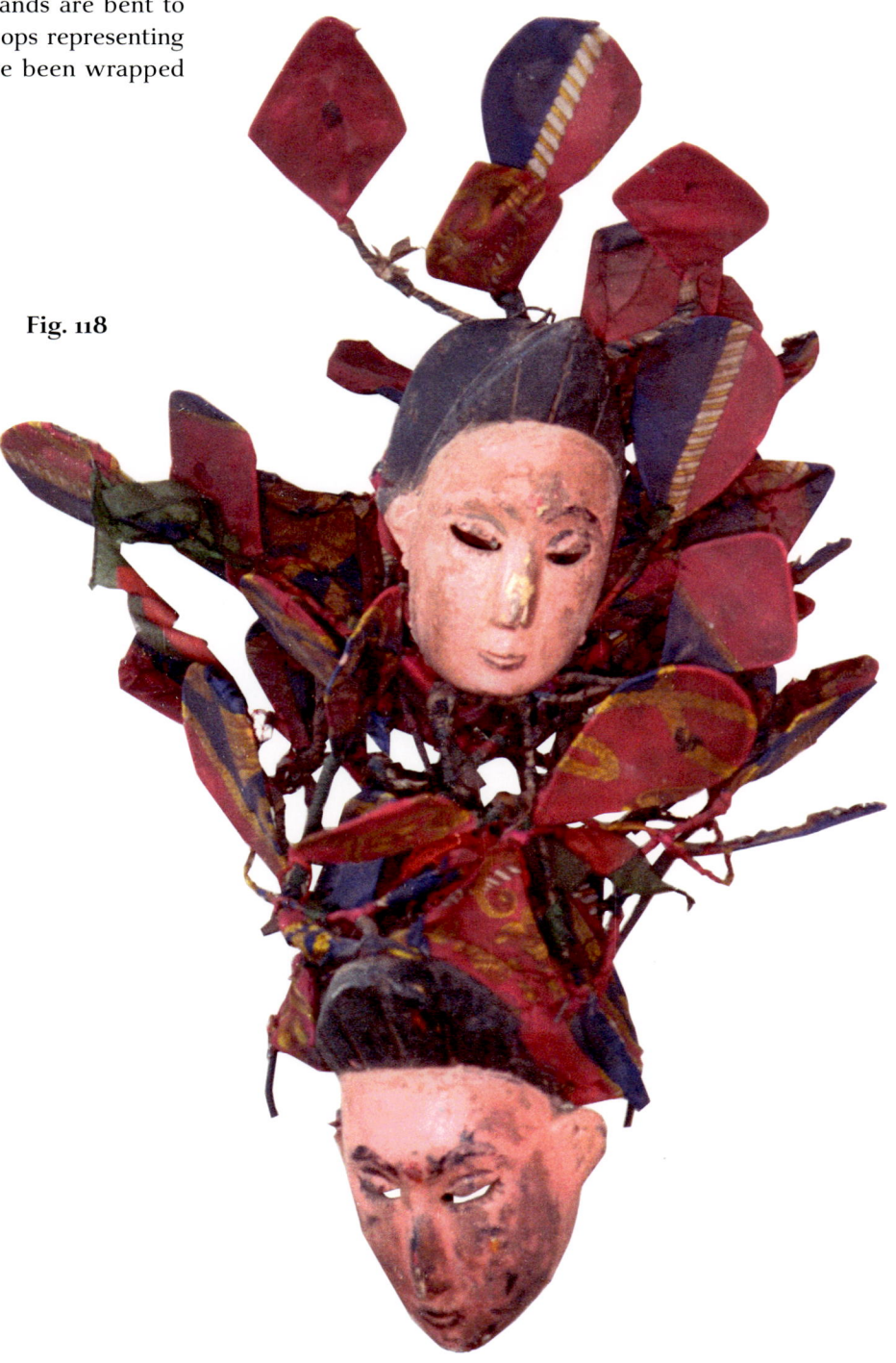

Fig. 118

Fig. 119

FACE MASK
Temne People: Sierra Leone
Materials: *Wood, paint, cloth, fiber.*
H 32 in.

This extraordinary tri-level Ode-Lay Society mask carved from a single block of wood has prominent Hindu-inspired, Mami Wata features in the lower face and the upper female figure holding two snakes **(Fig. 119)**. The middle portion is comprised of three fierce leopard heads with protruding tongues and exposed teeth. Arising on either side from behind the lower mask are two snakes that are attacking the large, central leopard head **(Fig. 120)**.

Fig. 120

Fig. 121

FACE MASK *(Dege)*
Dogon People: Mali
Materials: *Wood, pigment.*
H 16 in.

This mask with large, vertical rectangular eyes and a domed forehead represents a monkey, sometimes described as a baboon. It appears during funeral rites *(dama)* and at mourning ceremonies to conduct the deceased to their place among the ancestors. The masker, hidden beneath a vest of blackened palm fibers, carries a stick and moves with the gait of a monkey. The mask seeks to soothe and placate the spirits of the recently dead.

Fig. 122

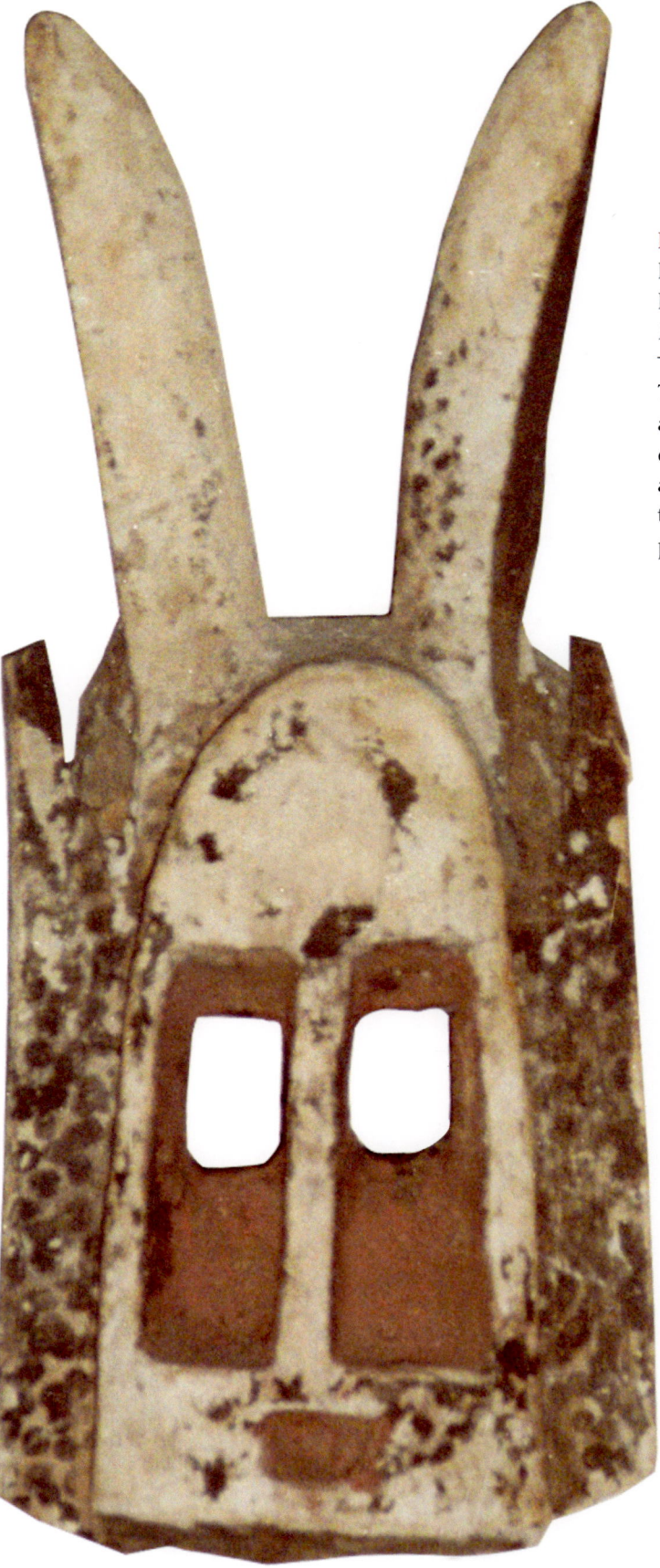

FACE MASK (*Walu*)
Dogon People: Mali
Materials: *Wood, pigment.*
H 11.5 in.

The *Walu* mask representing an antelope has vertical, rectangular eyes surmounted by a pair of horns and ears. The masker carries a stick that he uses to scratch the soil as if planting grain.

Fig. 123

Fig. 124

Fig. 125

Fig. 126

HEAD CREST MASKS (Chi Wara)
Bamana People: Mali
Materials: *Wood, pigment, metal, seeds, leather, hair.*
Fig. 123: *H 17 in.;* Fig. 124: *H 22 in.;* Fig. 125: H 40 in.; Fig. 126: *H 11 in., W 21 in.*

The Bamana people are predominantly farmers who live chiefly in central Mali. The *Chi wara* head crest mask represents the mythical roan antelope *(Hippotragus equinus)* that the Bamana believe taught them to farm. The antelope is a metaphor for the farmer since the curve of its neck when grazing is similar to the curve of the farmer's back as he bends over wielding a hoe in his fields. These masks appear at the beginning and end of the annual farming cycle. The dance imitates the movements of antelopes thereby symbolizing the effort, strength, and energy of the successful farmer. A costume of blackened plant fibers covers the entire body of the dancer who holds a stick representing the antelope's foreleg in each hand. The wood head crest is attached to a small basket cap that is affixed to the dancer's head.

Different forms of *Chi wara* predominate in various regions of Mali corresponding to agricultural areas. Head crests from central and eastern Mali have a vertical orientation with upright horns **(Fig. 125)**, whereas those from the northwest are typically horizontal **(Fig. 126)**. In southern and southwestern Mali, one finds a vertical, abstract, composite form **(Figs. 123, 124)**. In addition to horns representing an antelope, all three forms incorporate elements of the aardvark, the pangolin, or both. Vertical *Chi wara* are carved from a single piece of wood **(Figs. 123, 124, 125)**, whereas the horizontal *Chi wara* consists of a separately carved head and body joined by metal staples **(Fig. 126)**. The aardvark and pangolin appear in some *Chi wara* masks because they are admired for their determination and skill as diggers. Typically, the aardvark is at the bottom of the carving, the pangolin in the center, and the antelope represented by horns is at the top in the headdress. The composite form embodies the ideal farmer with the strength of the antelope and the digging skill of the pangolin and aardvark.

Chi wara dance in pairs representing a male and female antelope. In so doing, they express the essential roles of male (sun) and female (earth) elements in human and agricultural fertility, while at the same time encouraging cooperation between young men and women in cultivating the soil, planting, and hoeing. Champion male farmers are selected to wear the head crests in a dance that is accompanied by male drummers and a chorus of women. The male *Chi wara* is trailed by the female who imitates its steps to an accelerating rhythm that climaxes in motions that imitate the leaping of an antelope. The horns refer to millet, and the baby on a female *Chi wara* symbolizes human beings. Water, the other essential ingredient for successful farming, is represented by the black plant fiber costume worn with the headdress.

Fig. 127

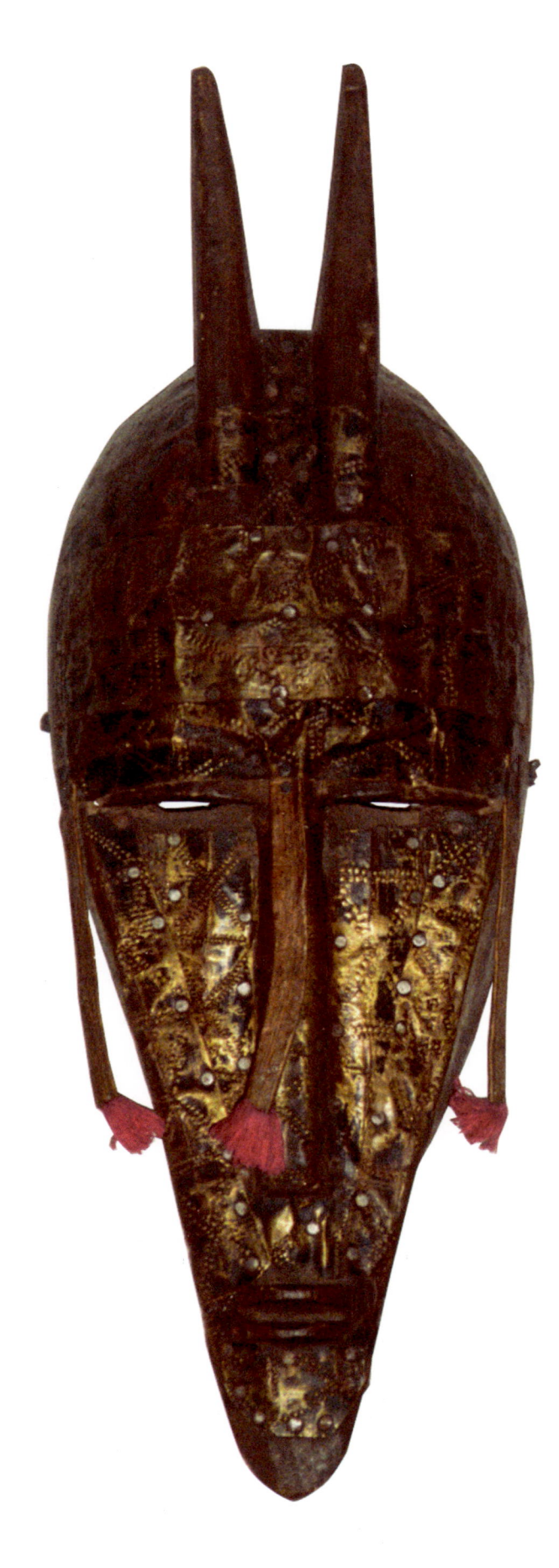

FACE MASK
Marka People:
Mali; Burkina Faso
Materials: *Wood, brass, cotton.*
H 16.5 in.

This mask is worn during initiation ceremonies for young boys as well as at festivals related to hunting and fishing. It is usually sheathed in hammered brass (as here) or aluminum sheet metal that is attached with small nails. The horns on top are an allusion to a male antelope. Metal strips representing braids tied with red cotton threads hang on either side of the face and in front of the nose.

Fig. 128

HELMET CREST MASK *(Djimini)*
Senufo People: Mali; Ivory Coast
Materials: *Wood, pigment.*
H 22.5 in.

The Senufo people live in the Ivory Coast and adjacent areas of Mali. This very uncommon mask was obtained from Senufo people in Mali. It displays an eagle and two subsidiary eaglets. The eagle is considered to be the king of birds and a superb fisherman. The mask is thought to have been used by a society of hunters or fishermen, possibly to denote the authority of elders. The large eagle may represent the elders as guardians of their younger counterparts metaphorically standing out on limbs. The following unexplained inscription is painted on the dorsum of the eagle's tail: *na bè da la* **(Fig. 129)**.

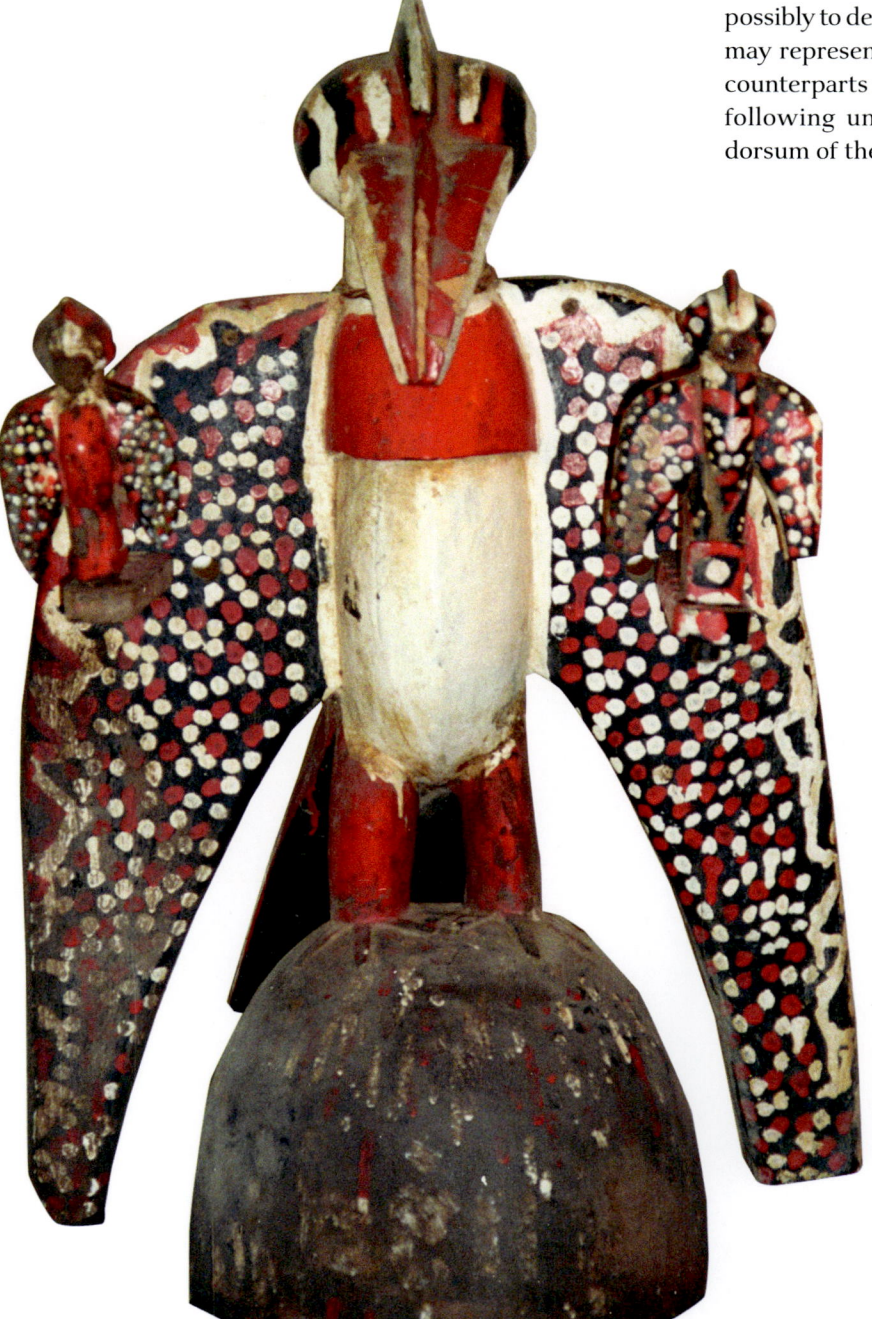

Fig. 129

PLANK MASKS
Tusyan (Tussian) Or Siemu People: Burkina Faso
Materials: *Wood, pigment, mirrors, waxy compound, Abrus precatorius seeds, plant fibers.*
Fig. 130: *H 38.5 in., W 22.5 in.*; Fig. 131: *H 43 in., W 23 in.*

These plank masks are danced when adolescent boys are initiated into the *Do* cult. As part of the ceremony, initiates are given new secret names associated with birds and wild animals. The animal name reflects the boy's character and becomes his personal emblem. The bird head attached to both of these masks probably represents the grey hornbill, *Tockus nasutus*. One mask **(Fig. 130)** is topped by the horns of a buffalo *(kab* or *kap)*, one of the highest levels of initiation because it is a powerful animal associated with leadership and prestige. Whereas buffalo horns are usually carved from the plank that forms the face of the mask, the head of an animal is typically carved separately and attached to the plank either on the surface using adhesive material or into a flange at the top of the mask **(Fig. 131)**. The face of the mask is often decorated with a large X made from adherent waxy material into which red *Abrus* seeds have been embedded. Mirrors in the eyes may be intended to connect the wearer to deities of the *Do* spirit world.

Fig. 131

Fig. 130

Masks of The Voltaic People in Burkina Faso

Wooden masks, representing spirits who are important to the history of a clan or village, are worn by many groups of people inhabiting Burkina Faso, including the Bobo, Bwa, Mossi, Nuna, Winiama, and others. The masks bring spirits to life and are called upon to explain events or to solve problems such as famine, infertility, or illness. The masks are usually carved for a family or clan at the direction of a diviner who has been consulted about a particular situation. Spirits who may be responsible for the difficulty or are thought to have the capacity to intervene are represented by the masks. Spirits known to inhabit animals, such as a buffalo, bird, or snake, are represented by masks carved in naturalistic forms. Abstract masks, such as a disc or a disc combined with a plank, are used for spirits not embodied by animals. Composite masks incorporating animal and human features, or features of two different animals, represent spirits who are called upon to deal with certain issues because they have special powers.

    The surfaces of all masks used by these ethnic groups are decorated with geometric designs that may be carved and/or painted on the surface. Until recently, these patterns were outlined in red, white, and black pigments mixed with clay. Black may be obtained from boiled acacia seed pods, red from iron-rich clay, and white from lizard excrement. In some instances, commercial paints are now used. The patterns are referred to as "scars" because they duplicate the complex cutaneous scarifications that were a traditional adornment, a custom no longer practiced. Constituting the language of the spirits, the symbols are taught to children at the time of their initiation into adulthood. The character of a particular mask is expressed by its form and the movements of its dance.

Fig. 132

FACE MASK *(Wan-Zega)*
Mossi People: Burkina Faso
Materials: *Wood, paint. H 31.5 in.*

This mask is from the eastern Mossi people in the Boulsa region. The post on top of the mask was sheathed in layers of plant fibers, and the performer wore a costume woven from the same fibers. Three types of masks participate in the event. The spike on top of a male mask is covered with plant fibers that are dyed red, and fibers of the same color are used to create the costume. Black plant fibers have the same distribution on female masks. A third, shorter mask representing a child has two horns on top that are also sheathed in plant fibers. The three masks represent a family of bush spirits who appear at a funeral to escort the deceased person to the spirit world. They also appear at initiation rites and at celebrations when the spirits of the ancestors are called upon to bless the community. The male and female masks are worn by adult men, and the children's mask is worn by a boy. Since male and female masks are both painted white and are sculpturally similar, the gender of the mask illustrated here without a costume cannot be determined.

FACE MASK (*Wan-Balinga*)
Mossi People: Burkina Faso
Materials: *Wood, pigment, plant fibers.*
H 19 in. without hair.

This mask is thought to represent a Fulani woman. The hair is formed by rope-like strands of braided plant fibers.

Fig. 133

HEAD CREST MASK (*Wan-Noraogo*)
Mossi People: Burkina Faso
Materials: *Wood, pigment. H 18.5 in.*

This mask depicts a rooster and is worn on top of the head. The person dancing the mask is entirely covered by a cloak of long, dark red or black plant fibers. The ribbed crest on top of the mask represents the rooster's cockscomb. The mask appears at agricultural celebrations.

Fig. 134

HEAD CREST MASK
Bwa People: Burkina Faso
Materials: *Wood, pigments. H 17 in.*

This mask represents the buffalo, a village spirit that played an important role in the history of the community. The bird on its crown is probably an ox pecker that picks insects from the buffalo's back and warns it of approaching danger. The mask is worn on top of the head, pitched at an angle that allows the wearer to see through the triangular snout. It is held in place by a hood of netted fiber, and the performer wears a hemp costume that is dyed red or black.

Fig. 135

Fig. 136

FACE MASK
Nunuma People: Burkina Faso
Materials: *Wood, pigment, rope.
H 12 in.*

The alert ears thrust forward and the toothsome mouth of a hyena, an important village spirit, are captured by this mask that is worn tipped up so that the wearer can see through the mouth. The performer darts around furtively and runs aggressively at the audience.

Fig. 137

103

Fig. 138

Fig. 139

FACE MASK (*Kê Duneh*)
Winiama People: Burkina Faso
Materials: *Wood, pigment. H 22.5 in.*

This mask has a single flat horn that curves backward to form an almost complete circle. It represents a wild, entranced bush spirit that moves unsteadily and may strike at people in its path. The masker is shrouded by a voluminous costume that includes red plant fibers. A peg at the base of the mask is a handle that is used by the performer to stabilize and adjust the mask during the dance.

Fig. 140

PLANK MASK
Nuna or Winiama People:
Burkina Faso
Materials: *Wood, pigments.*
H 59 in.

The tall, tapering vertical element rising above the face mask represents an eel. The oval face with triangular eyes separated by a vertical crest is a characteristic feature of this type of mask. Carved geometric designs highlighted with red, white, and brown pigments decorate the body of the eel. The people who carve these masks believe that human life begins in the form of an eel swimming in the mother's womb. Ritual sacrifices are made to sacred eels kept in a pond near a village in order to enhance human fertility and agricultural abundance. Because of its association with fertility, the eel is the first mask to appear in festivals celebrating the start of the rainy season when planting begins.

Fig. 141

PLANK MASK
Bwa People: Burkina Faso
Materials: *Wood, pigment. H 11 in. W 58 in.*

This horizontal, winged plank mask represents a bird or a butterfly. It embodies the spirit of nature, symbolizing the awakening of growth brought about by rain after the dry period. Masks such as this appear at initiation ceremonies, at funerals, and for entertainment.

HELMET MASK (*Nwenke*)
Bobo People: Burkina Faso
Materials: *Wood, paint, string. H 47 in.*

Stylized, sacred masks of this type are carved by blacksmiths for use in initiations. They represent a spirit rather than a human or animal figure. The long, trapezoidal face tapers at the bottom to a narrow chin **(Fig. 142)**. The nose and rounded brow come together to form a T between the small, square eye holes. The nose is represented by an elongated sagittal crest extending from the brow nearly to the lower tip of the mask. Ears are indicated by small, slightly concave wooden blocks on either side, lateral to the eyes. A mobile, semi-lunar attachment that swings from side to side has been tied to the sagittal crest where it extends over the forehead to the dome of the helmet **(Fig. 143)**.

The upper two-fifths of the mask is a complex, rectangular, vertical plank with triangular perforations. The lower corners of the plank hang down on either side of the helmet but are not attached to it. A rectangular 9-inch x 4-inch, two-tiered box is firmly attached to the front of the plank just above the dome of the helmet **(Figs. 142, 143)**. The sides of the box are pierced by three round holes in each tier. A short wooden cylinder rises from the top. The box resembles a house or an old-fashioned riverboat, but we do not know what it is intended to represent. The word "bato" has been inscribed on the back of the plank behind the box **(Fig. 144)**. The meaning of this word is uncertain without field information because writing on masks is often very specific and individualized.

The surfaces of the mask, including the plank, are decorated with complex patterns created with red, green and yellow enamel paint on a white background. The designs consist mostly of triangles and diamonds formed from pairs of triangles that represent *sebe* or amulets with magical properties. *Nwenke* masks are repainted each season. The performer wears a costume made from hemp fibers.

Fig. 142

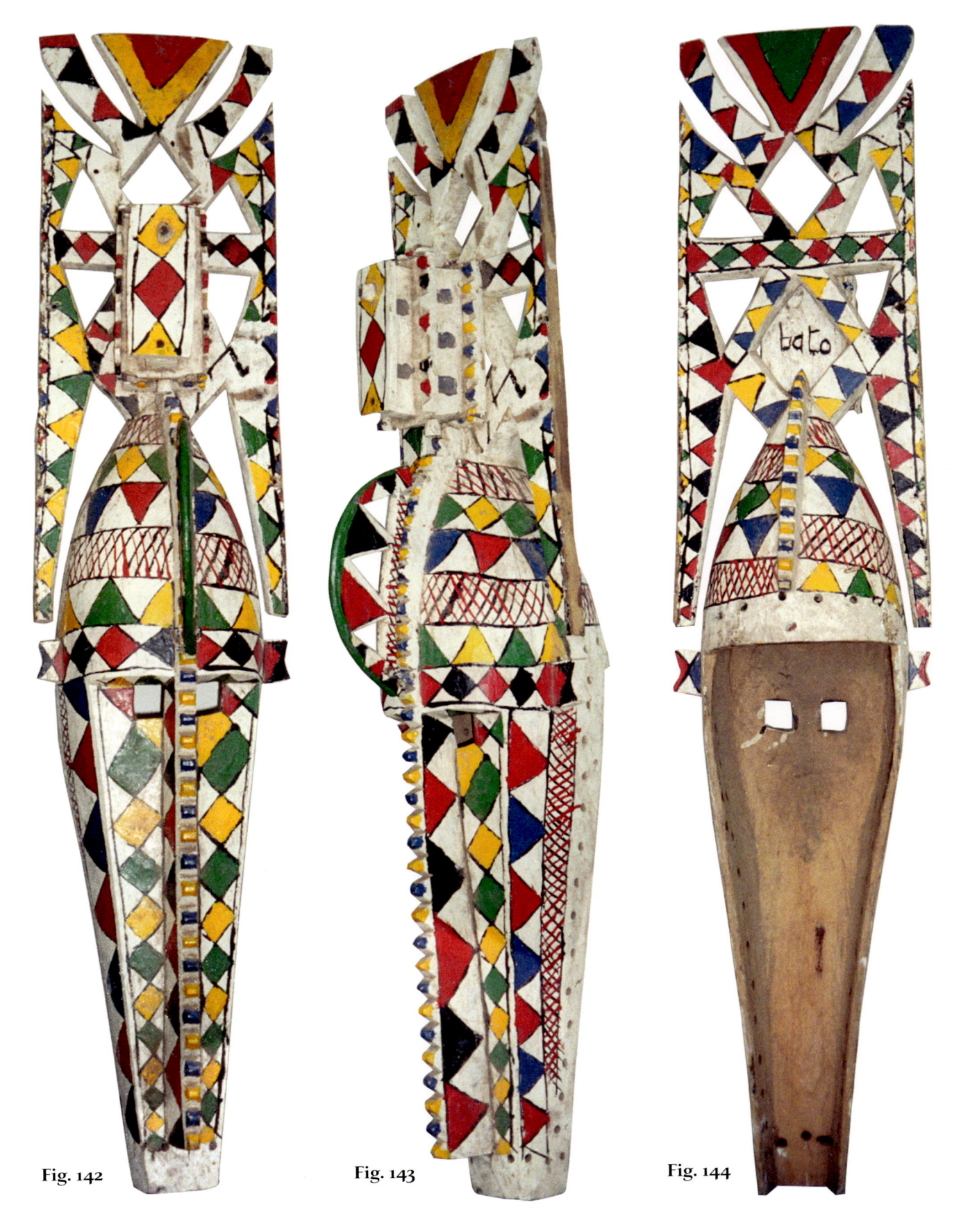

Fig. 143

Fig. 144

107

Elu Face Masks of the Ogoni People in Nigeria

The Ogoni people living in the eastern Niger River delta have multiple men's societies that perform religious and social functions in which they employ small masks *(Elu* or *Nyalu)* with articulated jaws. The masker is able to open the jaw and snap it shut with an audible click by movements of his mouth. Many, but not all, of these masks have prominent teeth made from cane sticks implanted in the jaw. The teeth are visible when the jaw is opened. Raised scarifications are sometimes carved on the forehead and temples of the masks. Other typical features are the full lips, narrow eyes, and snub nose. Female masks can be identified by their elaborate coiffure, and male masks sometimes mimic a men's European hairstyle. Objects perched on top of the head are emblems of specific societies or refer to the subject of the masquerade. The masks, held in place by a textile and plant fiber hood, appear at funerals and during harvest festivals. The upper body of the masker is covered by a raffia costume. *Elu* masks can be caricatures of members of the community. The masquerades illustrate humorous, happy, and tragic events recorded in oral traditions and songs as well as offering commentary on recent events.

Fig. 145

FACE MASK (*Elu*)
Ogoni People: Nigeria
Materials: *Wood, pigment.*
H 10.5 in.

The hairstyle of this female mask consists of a central, conical tower and two lateral, hanging braids. Teeth are present in the mouth.

Fig. 146

Fig. 147

FACE MASK (*Elu*)
Ogoni People: Nigeria
Materials: *Wood, pigment. H 10 in.*

This female mask displays the flat top, tower hairstyle. No teeth are present in the mouth.

FACE MASK (*Elu*)
Ogoni People: Nigeria
Materials: *Wood, pigment. H 11 in.*

The hair on this mask is arranged in two horn-like braids. There are no teeth in the mouth.

Fig. 148

Fig. 149

FACE MASK *(Elu)*
Ogoni People: Nigeria
Materials: *Wood, pigment. H 9.5 in.*

This mask has a wavy hairstyle with a central knob. Teeth are present in the mouth.

FACE MASK *(Elu)*
Ogoni People: Nigeria
Materials: *Wood, pigment. H 8 in.*

This mask has an articulated jaw without teeth. Black pigment highlights the wide eyes, the lips, and a vertical band on the forehead. The coiffure has an unusual angular configuration.

Fig. 150

Fig. 151

FACE MASK (*Elu*)
Ogoni People: Nigeria
Materials: *Wood, pigment. H 8 in.*

This mask has a man's pompadour hairstyle. There are teeth in the mouth.

FACE MASK (*Elu*)
Ogoni People: Nigeria
Materials: *Wood, pigment. H 9 in.*

The box-like object on top of this mask is probably an amulet. The mask does not have teeth.

Fig. 152

FACE MASK (*Elu*)
Ogoni People: Nigeria
Materials: *Wood, pigment. H 13 in.*

A calabash is situated on top of this female mask. The hairstyle includes braids hanging on either side of the face that are similar to the coiffure on the mask in **Fig. 145**. The pursed lips and sloping, pointed nose seen in the side view are characteristic features of Ogoni *Elu* masks. The mask has teeth.

Fig. 153

113

Fig. 154

Fig. 155

FACE MASK (*Elu*)
Ogoni People: Nigeria
Materials: *Wood, pigment. H 7.5 in.*

This men's mask is outfitted with a black derby hat. There are no teeth in the mouth.

FACE MASK (*Elu*)
Ogoni People: Nigeria
Materials: *Wood, pigment. H 7 in.*

This men's mask features a pith helmet, prominent rectangular ears, and a cross-shaped mark on the forehead. The articulated mouth lacks teeth.

Fig. 156

Fig. 157

FACE MASK (*Elu*)
Ogoni People: Nigeria
Materials: *Wood, pigment. H 7.5 in.*

This brown men's mask wears a pith helmet. The mask does not have teeth.

FACE MASK (*Elu*)
Ogoni People: Nigeria
Materials: *Wood, pigment. H 9 in.*

This *Nzopie* or singing ghost mask has a mouth shaped like a bird beak. Teeth are present in the mouth.

Fig. 158

Fig. 159

FACE MASK (*Elu*)
Ogoni People: Nigeria
Materials: *Wood, pigment. H 9 in.*

This brown-faced mask has abundant hair that has been combed to one side. Teeth are present in the articulated mouth.

FACE MASK (*Elu*)
Ogoni People (?): Nigeria
Materials: *Wood, pigment. H 16.5 in.*

This mask has an articulated jaw, teeth carved in the gums, prominent frontal scarification, and dark pigmentation. It is larger than the majority of Ogoni *Elu* masks. The square object carved on the front of the cap above the frontal scarification could be an amulet. This mask may belong to one of the ethnic groups living near the Ogoni who sometimes used masks with a mobile lower jaw.

Fig. 160

Fig. 161

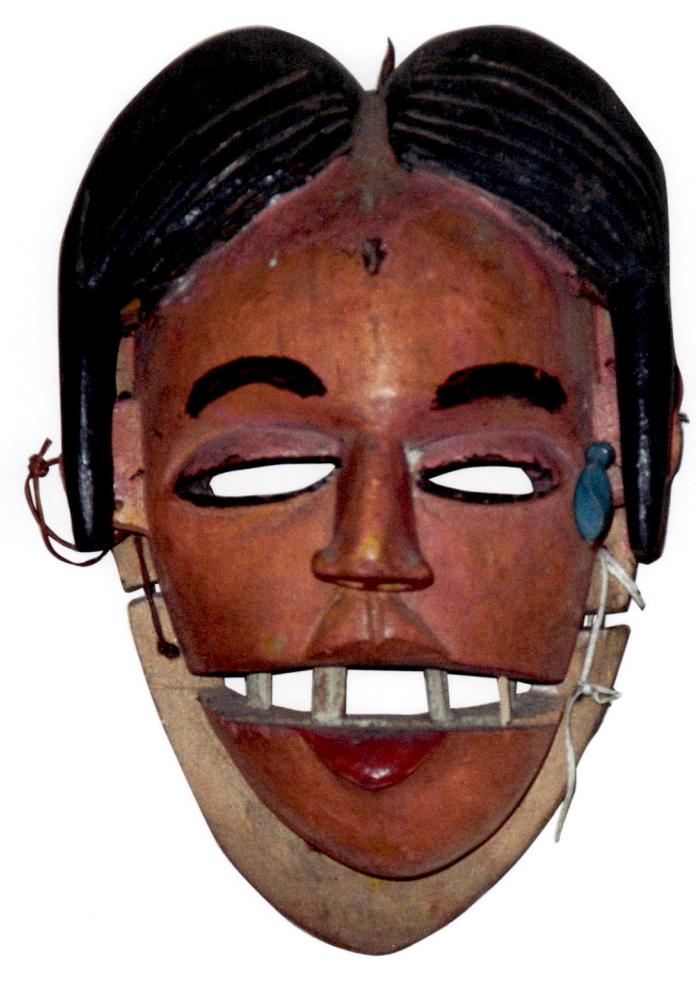

FACE MASK (*Elu*)
Ogoni People (?): Nigeria
Materials: *Wood, pigment. H 11 in.*

This mask with a hinged jaw and a multitude of thin teeth has a brown face and a blackened, spiked hairstyle. The mask is slightly larger than the typical Ogoni *Elu* mask and may belong to an ethnic group living near the Ogoni who sometimes used masks with a moveable jaw.

FACE MASK (*Elu*)
Ogoni People (?): Nigeria
Materials: *Wood, paint, beads. H 9 in.*

When opened, the hinged jaw of this mask reveals four relatively broad teeth. Other unusual features are the face painted orange and the beaded earrings. This mask was used by the Ogoni people or one of the neighboring ethnic groups.

Fig. 162

FACE MASK (*Karikpo*)
Ogoni People: Nigeria
Materials: *Wood, pigment.*
H 32 in.

Worn during rituals that honor ancestors and ancestral deities at the beginning of agricultural festivals, horned masks of the *Karikpo* society mimic the darting movements of the bushbuck antelope.

Fig. 163

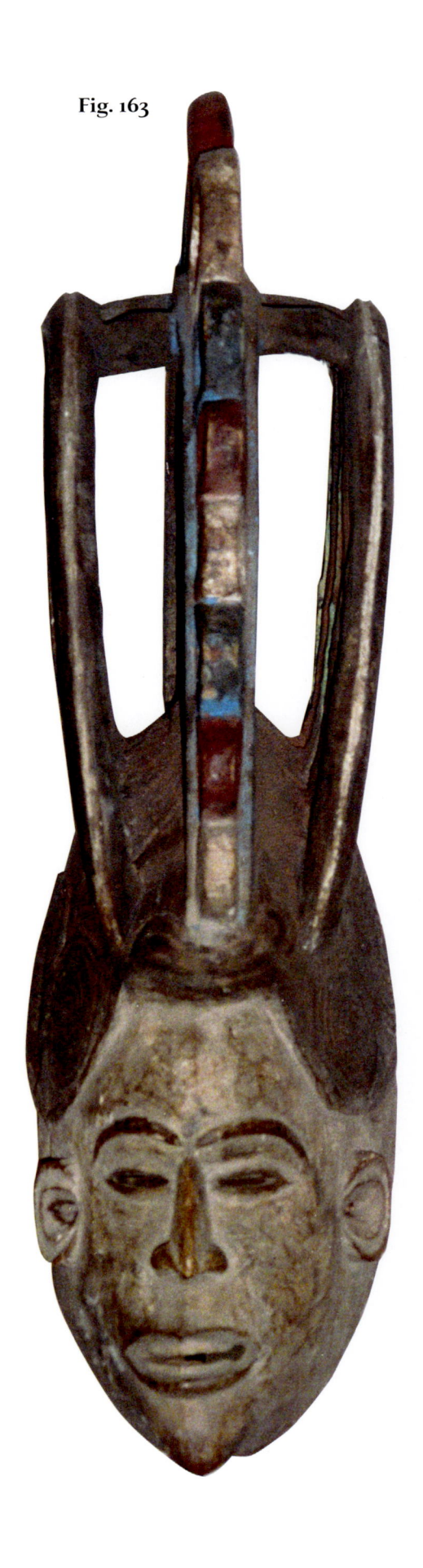

Fig. 164

HELMET MASK (*Mmwo*)
Igbo (Ibo) People: Nigeria
Materials: *Wood, pigment. H 24 in.*

The maiden spirit mask used by the *Mmwo* Society embodies the spirit of a female ancestor as well as the physical and moral beauty of the ideal young woman. It has a carved representation of the traditional crested hairstyle worn by unmarried women. In reality, the coiffure was modeled with clay around an armature and supported by combs, mirrors, and other attachments. In the example illustrated here, discs and rings on either side of the central crest represent combs used to stabilize the coiffure or coins that were attached to the hair. The long, straight nose, small mouth, and elaborate hairstyle depict the ideal of feminine beauty, while the white face is a reference to the ancestors.

The *Mmwo* mask worn by an initiated man in his 30s to 50s performs at the Agbogho festival to celebrate the beauty of young women, the importance of the family unit, and to support community values. The mask appears at festivals and funerals to perform a dance that imitates the graceful, dignified movement of an ideal, young Igbo woman who is a proud representative of her family and a potential source of bridewealth.

Fig. 165

MMWO COSTUME
Igbo (Ibo) People : Nigeria
Materials: *Cloth. H 67 in.*

This tight-fitting body suit with colorful embroidered and appliquéd designs is worn by a male maiden spirit mask (*Mmwo*) performer. Cotton sport stockings worn on the hands and feet have become frayed through use. The decorative motifs named after natural and man-made objects or concepts are based on body painting designs (*ùli* or *ùri*) used by Igbo men and women. Tubular, bullet-shaped breasts and an umbilicus made from cloth are attached to the costume **(Fig. 166)**.

Fig. 166

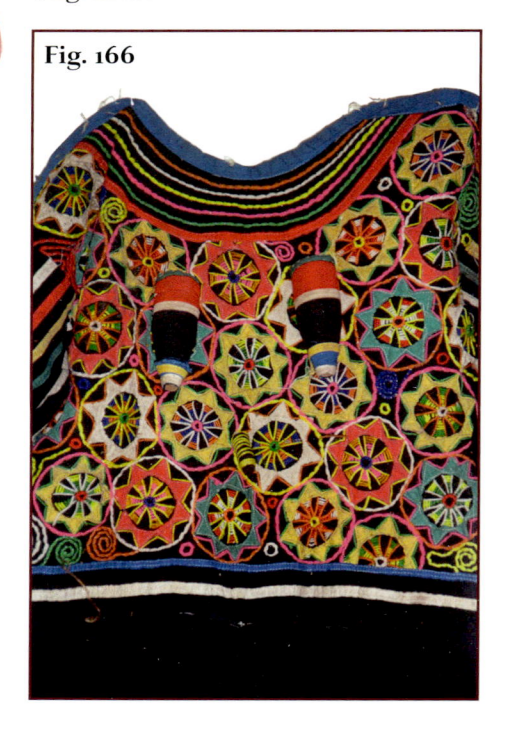

Fig. 167

FACE MASK (*Okoroshia*)
Igbo (Ibo) People: Nigeria
Materials: *Wood, pigment. H 12 in.*

This female mask displays hair with a central part that has been pulled upward into two symmetrical horn-like braids arching over the serene white face. The use of white in this situation is associated with beauty and femininity in contrast to red and black that indicate maleness and aggressive qualities.

The Igbo horned hairstyle was described as follows by G.I. Jones in his book, *Ibo Art*:

Younger women usually kept their hair close to their head. ...On more special occasions (for example, before marriage or after the birth of their first baby) they trained it out and tied it into long, curved "horns."

The hairstyle depicted on the mask and more elaborate ornamental hairstyles molded with clay and oil were considered to be signs of wealth since they showed that the family could spare the daughter from heavy labor and carrying loads on her head while she had this coiffure.

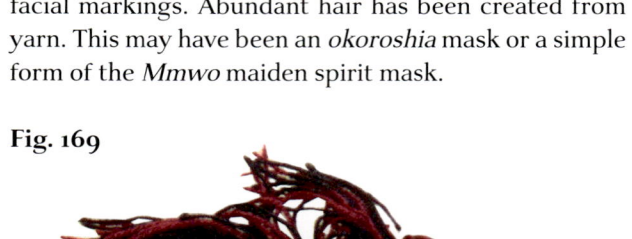

FACE MASK
Igbo (Ibo) People: Nigeria
Materials: *Wood, paint, foam rubber. H 17 in.*

This regal, white-faced male mask, possibly representing an ancestral spirit, wears a crown. Diagonal slits in the cheeks are viewing holes since there are no apertures in the eyes. Masks such as this sometimes appear in pairs representing a king and queen. A small piece of foam rubber has been attached inside the top of the mask where it rested on the wearer's head.

Fig. 168

FACE MASK (*Okoroshia Or Mmwo*)
Igbo (Ibo) People: Nigeria
Materials: *Wood, pigment, yarn. H 10 in.*

This feminine white-faced mask is endowed with black facial markings. Abundant hair has been created from yarn. This may have been an *okoroshia* mask or a simple form of the *Mmwo* maiden spirit mask.

Fig. 169

Fig. 170

FACE MASK
Igbo (Ibo) People: Nigeria
Materials: *Wood, paint. H 8 in.*

The coiffure of this mask includes carved representations of large snails *(ejula)* that are a delicacy as well as symbols of coolness and femininity. When filled with plant material and other substances, the shells served as amulets that were attached to a woman's hair.

Fig. 171

HEAD CREST MASK
Izzi People: Nigeria
Materials: *Wood, paint. W 22 in.*

The Izzi are one of more than 30 subgroups of the Igbo (Ibo) people living in southeastern Nigeria. This composite mask, worn on top of the head, depicts a hyena attacking a snake with two chameleons as onlookers.

Head Crest Masks of the Ijo People

Amorphous water spirits that inhabit the world of the Ijo and other people who populate the Niger River delta manifest themselves in the form of aquatic animals, such as the shark, crocodile, python, hippo, and sawfish. They appear as masks in the *Owu* Society masquerade of the Ijo and neighboring people. The masks sometimes combine human and animal attributes. In his book *The Art of Eastern Nigeria,* G.I. Jones reported that the mythical origin of these masks is attributed "…to a man who went fishing on the Ijo day of rest. He saw the spirits dancing in the moonlight on a sand bar and persuaded them to come and repeat the performance in his village." Water creatures are unpredictable spirits capable of disrupting the routine of daily life or bringing good fortune to the community. The dance is intended to control and appease these powerful spirits.

An *Owu* mask belongs to the spirit it represents. It is kept in the meetinghouse of the *Owu* Society, except when it appears in a masquerade, sometimes rising from and returning to the water. Head crest masks are worn on top of the head because, as reported to G.I. Jones, "…this was the way that water spirits normally appeared to people, with their bodies hidden by the water and their faces level with its surface." The identity of a mask is indicated by the drum rhythm and music that accompany the performance when the spirit is said "to walk with" the dancer.

The styles of masks vary in different regions of the Niger Delta. In general, masks of animals are carved in a naturalistic, three-dimensional style. On the other hand, a human face is flattened on the upper surface of a narrow board and broken down into geometric components exemplified by eyes represented as solid cylinders. The shape of the board on which the face appears is carved as the abstract representation of an animal water spirit such as a fish. The masks are often embellished with white pigment because it is believed that water spirits are attracted to this color associated with ancestors who reside beneath the water **(Figs. 172, 173)**.

Fig. 172

Fig. 173

HEAD CREST MASK
Ijo People: Nigeria
Materials: *Wood, pigment, cloth.*
H 8 in. W 23.5 in.

This mask presents an abstracted representation of a human face on the upper surface of a board. The forked, pointed ends of the board refer to fish tails and the circular enlargement in the middle of the board might be the body of a turtle. The entire mask is coated with a thick layer of chalky, white pigment over a black undercoat. Slender hanging strips of red cloth form a fringe around the perimeter of the board.

Fig. 174

Fig. 175

HEAD CREST MASK
Ijo People: Nigeria
Materials: *Wood, pigment, basketry, cloth. W 36.5 in.*

This mask **(Fig. 174)** depicts a shark situated on a basketry base.

HEAD CREST MASK
Ijo People: Nigeria
Materials: *Wood, pigment, mirrors. W 29 in.*

The crocodile is one of the dangerous, powerful animals inhabiting the swamps in the Niger River delta that are represented in water spirit masquerades performed in Ijo villages. White pigment is often used to color these masks **(Fig. 175)** because of the belief that white is attractive to the spirits. Rectangular mirrors are attached to the sides of the crocodile.

Fig. 176

HEAD CREST MASK
Ijo People (?): Nigeria
Materials: *Wood, pigment, metal. W 17 in.*

This mask depicts a pirogue of the type used in the Niger delta where the Ijo people live. Since Africans, especially chiefs, sometimes wore European-style hats, the figures in the pirogue are probably a chief and the bearer of his spear or staff of authority.

Fig. 177

FACE MASK *(Otogho)*
Afikpo People: Nigeria
Materials: *Wood, pigment, raffia fibers. H 9 in.*

The Afkipo are a small subset of the Igbo people. Their homeland borders on the Cross River in northeastern central Nigeria. The Afikpo word for "mask *(ihu)* also means "face." This small mask is named *otogho*, meaning "to peck like a bird" or *otoghokpokpo* (woodpecker, where *kpo* refers to the pecking sound). The masquerader carries a special wooden machete, *obuke*, and the mask is sometimes identified by this name. He wears a raffia outfit. The dance is a commentary on a man who is too boastful.

Fig. 178

HEADDRESS MASK (*Egungun*)
Yoruba People: Nigeria
Materials: *Cloth, wood, metal, decorative material. H 60 in. W 40 in.*

Egungun masks appear during a festival held in each community to honor ancestors. The Yoruba expression for ancestor is the phrase, *Ara orum*, meaning "being from beyond" or "dwellers in heaven." The dead are viewed as continuing to exist in another realm and, as a consequence, the well being of the living depends on a harmonious relationship with their ancestors. During the festival, the "living dead" reappear in mask forms as the *Egungun* or "masked power" to assert their moral authority. The performer is concealed by the *Egungun* mask that serves to reveal the power of the ancestors and represents the reverence of the mask's owner for the dead.

This type of *Egungun* mask is probably from the Oyo region. The headpiece is a narrow 3- to 4-foot long wooden board balanced on the wearers' head from which are suspended long, colorful strips of cloth with appliquéd serrated edges that completely enclose the masker. The performer is able to see through a net suspended in front of his face. When the masker dances, the suspended strips have an undulating motion, and when he spins, the strips whirl around him. Amulets, mirrors, and other decorative objects may be attached to the cloth strips. Each year, new cloth strips are added to the outside and as a consequence the number of layers are a guide to the years of use. The dancer, possessed by the spirits of ancestors, speaks with a disguised voice.

Fig. 179

Fig. 180

Fig. 181

HEADDRESS MASK
Yoruba People: Nigeria
Materials: *Cloth, beads, decorative material. H 40 in.*

Masks of this type are danced by young initiated boys and men, ranging in age from their teens to their early 30s. The masks are referred to as *locust spirits* who appear as unruly swarms running about singing and dancing, causing mischief, and whipping one another. The outfits are very varied. The type shown here consists of a cloth head covering with an embroidered face and braided synthetic hair decorated with beads. Symmetrical strips of appliquéd, brightly colored cloth decorate the torso of the costume. Tubular, protruding cloth breasts are attached to the chest **(Fig. 181)**.

131

Fig. 182

FACE MASK *(Oloju-Fofaro)*
Yoruba: Nigeria
Materials: *Wood, pigment. H 31.5 in.*

Face masks, such as the one shown here, are rare among the Yoruba. Masks of this type were used by the Ekiti-Yoruba in northeastern Yoruba-land where they were carved in Osi-Ilorin by Bamgboshe, a master carver, or one of his students. The masks are referred to as *Oloju-fofaro*, meaning "the owner of deep-set eyes." They appear at the Ijeshu festival honoring the *orisha* or god of the town of Osi, at Epa festivals, and at yam harvest festivals. The central kneeling female figure wearing a crown is believed to be a priestess of *Oshun*, the goddess of curative medicinal waters. In one hand she holds a string of white cowrie shells, a symbol of wealth. The other hand rests on a small, kneeling female attendant who holds a container with offerings for the priestess. Traditionally, the dominant dark red pigment was obtained by grinding red ironstone in water or from camwood powder. White pigment was made from ground shells, black from soot, and blue from laundry bluing compound. After it was painted, the mask was coated with a waterproofing substance extracted from the *Euphorbia* cactus. The mask was washed and repainted before it appeared in a festival.

Fig. 183

Fig. 184

HELMET MASK (Epa)
Yoruba People: Nigeria
Materials: *Wood, pigment. H 18 in.*

Epa masks honor various important ancestral and cultural heroes of the Yoruba people who live in northeastern Nigeria. They often depict a hunter or warrior, sometimes seated on a horse, who uses iron weapons and is thus under the influence of *Ogun*, god of iron, fire and war. A mother with children may also be depicted. The figures are idealized representations of important persons or events. Specific people and situations may be referenced in songs during the performance. These masks carved from a single block of wood and weigh up to 100 pounds. They consist of two parts: a lower oversized helmet mask face with an open mouth through which the wearer can see and an upper elaborately carved super structure composed of human and animal figures. The face represents the spirit of a deceased ancestor in a generalized form in contrast to the world of the living depicted in the more detailed carving of the superstructure. *Epa* masks are commissioned by a family that then owns the mask and is responsible for maintaining it. The mask is kept in a household shrine where it receives libations and prayers. Before it is danced, the mask is washed and repainted. *Epa* masks appear at festivals dedicated to community well-being and prosperity

The *Epa* mask illustrated here depicts a chief with his retinue carved in the round on a platform situated above the mask's helmet component consisting of a head and face with stereotypical features. Three figures seen in the frontal view **(Fig. 184)** are, from left to right, the chief's drummer who announces the chief's arrival (seen in profile), the chief with a pointed staff in his left hand and his right foot resting on a sphere representing his role as protector of the community, and the kneeling chief's wife, who holds a covered bowl of offerings. The chief's head is shaved except for a braided strip in the center running from the front to the back. The kneeling wife of the chief has the *suku* or knotted hair coiffure in which braids are drawn together to form a knot on top of the head. Part of the chief's right hand that may have held an emblem of leadership is missing. The view from the rear shows three figures representing other aspects of the chief's power who are, from left to right, the bearers of his shield, his rifle and his bow and arrows **(Fig. 183)**.

Fig. 185

Fig. 186

HEAD CREST MASK
Yoruba People: Nigeria
Materials: *Wood, paint, flashlight bulbs. H 19 in.*

This unusual mask, thought to represent Mami Wata, is worn on the head pitched slightly downward over the forehead. Flashlight bulbs have been inserted in the eyes of the snake and the female face, possibly to suggest clairvoyance. The body of the long snake is coiled into a knot over the forehead of the mask, duplicating the bow behind it formed by the tied, floral headscarf. The woman's braided hair, pulled together by an orange tie, loops forward over the headscarf and knotted snake. The tied end of the hair resembles the Hindu forehead pendant found on some representations of Mami Wata. Elaborate cheek scarifications and a red forehead dot are present.

Yoruba Gelede Masks of Nigeria and Benin

Gelede is a Yoruba Men's Society dedicated to maintaining and advancing the prosperity of the members of the society and of the community. These goals are promoted by performing plays and dances according to traditions set by their ancestors. The *Gelede* festival has two phases performed, respectively, during the afternoon and at night. The daytime performances consist of a series of acts in which paired masked male members of the society appear outfitted in identical costumes composed of brightly colored cloth strips, metal anklets, and masks. The dancers move in unison to reflect teamwork. The masks sit like caps on top of the head, covering the upper part of the face. In some instances, the mask is seated so high on the head that it is a headdress, and the dancer's face is covered by a veil of netting. In contrast to the Egungun masquerade, the identity of the wearer of a *Gelede* mask is not concealed.

As many as 50 pairs of masked performers may appear in turn during a *Gelede* festival. Each pair has a different form of mask, and each is identified by a name related to the specific subject represented by the superstructure situated above the idealized female head and face that forms the cap-like base of the mask. Topics include various professions and jobs (policeman, barber), machines (airplane, motorcycle), animals (birds, snakes) fashion (hairstyles), music, politics, etc. Social or spiritual commentary that is the subject of the masquerade is explained by the mask, costume, type of dance, music, spoken words, and accompanying song. It is often necessary to experience a mask in the context of performance in order to appreciate the point of view that the mask presents on a particular topic. Important themes are the resolution of conflict through cooperation and the avoidance of violence.

The central theme of the nocturnal *Gelede* masquerade is a celebration of the importance of women whose creative power through giving birth and nurturing children is necessary for the continued existence of the family and prosperity of the community. Women also have the potential for destructive power through witchcraft if they are barren. Female ancestors and elderly women (nearly ancestors) are especially revered. It is believed that if respected, women, through their inherent capacity to bear children, will protect and bless the community. Failure to respect and honor women can have disastrous consequences for the society. *Gelede* performances take place in the main market of a town, a site central to the social and economic power of women.

HEADDRESS MASK (Gelede)
Yoruba People: Nigeria
Materials: *Wood, pigment. H 8.5 in.*

This small brown mask might have been used by a boy learning to participate in the *Gelede* ceremony. It consists of a face topped by a simple cap partly painted black that is encircled by a snake.

Fig. 187

HEADDRESS MASK (Gelede)
Yoruba People: Benin
Materials: *Wood, paint. H 14 in.*

This brightly colored mask has the word "POBE" painted above the face, a reference to the town of Pobe in the country of Benin. The word "BINI" painted of the lion's flanks refers to Benin. The lion standing on the crown of the mask is a symbol of royal authority in Benin.

Fig. 188

HEADDRESS MASK *(Gelede)*
Yoruba People: Nigeria
Materials: *Wood, paint. H 15 in.*

This mask is surmounted by a complex, painted carving in which a bird accompanied by smaller birds on either side is attacking a snake. This might be a reference to a mother protecting her children.

Fig. 189

Fig. 190

Fig. 191

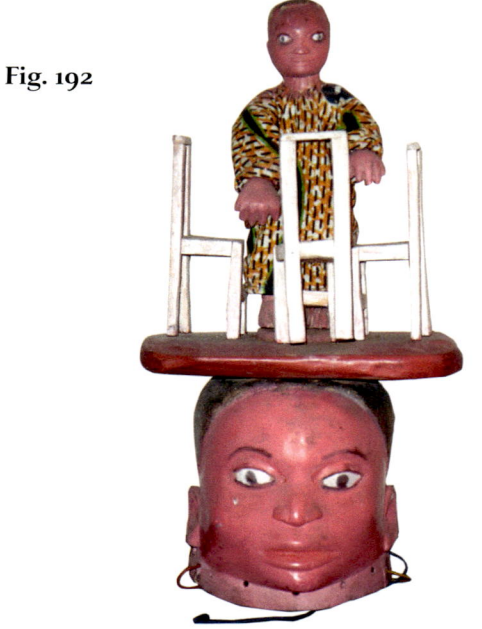

Fig. 192

Fig. 193

HEADDRESS MASKS (*Gelede Ero*)
Anago Yoruba People: Nigeria; Benin
Materials: *Wood, cloth, pigment, metal, string.*
Fig. 190: *H 16.5 in.*; Fig. 191: *H 15 in.*; Fig. 192: *H 17.5 in.*; Fig. 193: *H 14 in.*

The Anago Yoruba people live along the coast of southeastern Benin and southwestern Nigeria. Their *Gelede* masks include puppets called *ero*, meaning "machine magic," that are mounted on a wooden board attached to the top of a traditional *Gelede* mask. Many of the puppets are articulated by strings, but some are set in motion by the dancer's movements. The puppets depict serious and comic activities or scenes, often reflecting current events. The meaning of the mask is often kept secret ("awo") until it is explained in performance by accompanying songs or spoken commentary.

The outstretched wings of a bird standing on top of one mask can be made to flap by pulling a string that passes through a leg into the mask **(Fig. 190)**. The mask showing what appear to be two "acrobats" represents a child (smaller figure) being raised by its father **(Fig. 191)**. It speaks to the responsibility that fathers have in raising their children. When the string is pulled, the child is literally raised above his father's shoulders. The stories associated with the mask showing a man standing amidst four chairs **(Fig. 192)** and the mask with a recumbent man who can be raised to a seated position **(Fig. 193)** are not known to us. Since there is no written text, the meaning of a particular mask may be obscure out of the context of the performance and lost over time. *Ero* masks appear as entertainment during daytime *Gelede* performances in advance of important nocturnal *Efe* ceremonies.

Face Masks of the Anang (Ibibio) People

The Anang are a subgroup of the Ibibio people whose cultural center is around the commercially important Ikot Akpene region in Akwa Abom State between the Niger River Delta and Cross River area of coastal southeastern Nigeria. As reported to us by Eli Bentor, Professor of Art History at Appalachian State University, who has studied mask traditions in this region,

Ikot Ekpene is today the largest producer of masks throughout the larger area supplying Ibibio, Igbo, Cross River and Niger Delta communities… I have seen similar masks being carved in the market at Enugu (another town in this region)…The style is loosely based on older Ibibio face masks…. These masks are clearly used in festivals and burial ceremonies throughout the region….

Masks used in Southeast Nigeria today are frequently decorated with bright commercial paint that has been employed in this area for many decades.

Some of the illustrated masks display representations of Mami Wata or "mother of water," a water spirit associated with snakes. Mami Wata conflates the European concept of a mermaid who rises from the water with the exotic images of a snake charmer, Hindu deities and other influences. Many of the masks have the forehead dot that protects against the "evil eye." A rubber strap made from the inner tube of a bicycle tire fastened to the back of the mask is used to hold it over the wearer's face.

G.I. Jones, who studied art and culture in this area of Nigeria, noted that the masks have features "more reminiscent of the masks of Ceylon or Southern India than of traditional Anang (Ibibio) sculpture." In addition to Mami Wata, the masks depict subjects such as football (soccer) players, horses and/or eagles that draw upon aspects of the Nigerian coat of arms, and various other animals of probable metaphorical significance (e.g., scorpion, owl).

Color used to decorate these masks has symbolic significance. Light colors, such as white, pink, and yellow, are associated with daytime, beauty, wealth, positive feelings, and ancestors. Red, black, and brown are dark colors indicative of evil, ugliness and dangerous spirits. G.I. Jones reported in 1984 that, "Most Ibibio masks, until the 1930s, were stained and polished black, in the case of the fierce ones, or coloured white or white and light brown with local pigments. The more modern ones were coloured with imported and mainly oil paints of the colours that found favor in other parts of Eastern Nigeria."

Fig. 194

FACE MASK
Anang (Ibibio) People: Nigeria
Materials: *Wood, paint. H 21 in.*

The superstructure of this unusual mask **(Fig. 195)** depicts a Christ figure on a cross that is attached to an inscribed arch. Some of the text is faded but appears to consist of the following words: *Mr. Najime Ishermber. gaav Mba. Yeea. Va. Ve.* The reference to Christ reflects the prevalence of Christianity in southern Nigeria. Masks that depict Christian themes are uncommon in West Africa where Islam is the dominant religion.

Fig. 195

FACE MASK
Anang (Ibibio) People: Nigeria
Materials: *Wood. H 18.5 in.*

This unfinished mask **(Fig. 194)** reveals how the carver creates a face mask surmounted by a snake with a gaping mouth. The face is largely finished with well-formed ears, eyes, nose, and mouth. The surface of the face has been discolored by some inadvertently applied pink paint. The snake remains in the block form of an earlier stage of the process.

Fig. 196

FACE MASK
Anang (Ibibio) People: Nigeria
Materials: *Wood, paint, mirrors, nails, rubber. H 19.5 in.*

On this mask, a kneeling man with outstretched arms dressed in a white robe is holding posts topped by a star and crescent moon. The man may be a member of the New Age Christian religious sect, The Brotherhood of the Cross and Star, whose members wear white robes that they call *soutane* and meet in churches they identify as *bethels*. Since its origin in Calabar, Nigeria, in 1956, it has been led by Olumba Olumba Obu, who is described as the "Sole Spiritual Head of the Universe." The Brotherhood of the Cross and Star now has a world-wide distribution.

Serpentine appendages attached with nails to either side of the mask each hold two, small, round mirrors. The band of black rubber from the inner tube of a bicycle tire is attached to the back of the mask.

Fig. 197

FACE MASK
Anang (Ibibio) People: Nigeria
Materials: *Wood, paint.*
H 22.5 in.

This attractively painted mask depicts a pair of female sirens with fish-tail lower extremities. One upper extremity is depicted as a large fin and the other upper extremity is represented by a stunted arm. A snake arched over the top joins the figures. The painted motifs on the figures, their mermaid-like features, and the presence of a snake suggest that this mask is devoted to the water spirit, Mami Wata.

Fig. 198

FACE MASK
Anang (Ibibio) People: Nigeria
Materials: *Wood, paint. H 20 in.*

The superstructure of this mask **(Fig. 199)** consists of a man in shorts and a tee shirt who is kicking a ball with his right foot. With his right arm raised and his left arm lowered, he is steadying himself by holding on to a segmented arch that may represent a soccer goal. Decorative features on the face mask include a forehead dot and a pair of cheek dots.

Fig. 199

FACE MASK
Anang (Ibibio) People: Nigeria
Materials: *Wood, paint, beads, string, nails. H 20 in.*

On this mask **(Fig. 198)**, a man in a contemporary, Western-style jacket and long trousers stands on a snake. His legs are spread and his outstretched arms hold the upper part of the snake. The female face mask, including a forehead dot and multicolored beaded earrings has strong Hindu-inspired features. Flat, wooden appendages attached with nails to the sides of the face appear to be extensions of the mask's coiffure. The presence of a snake and the Hindu-inspired facial features suggest a reference to Mami Wata.

143

Fig. 200

FACE MASK
Anang (Ibibio) People: Nigeria
Materials: *Wood, paint, nails. H 28 in.*

The superstructure of this mask is a platform that supports two soccer players, each standing with one foot placed on top of a ball. The men, dressed in identical uniforms, evidently belong to the same team. The astonished looks on their faces may be due to the snake holding a soccer ball in its mouth that is wrapped around the players' heads and bodies. An inscription on the front edge of the platform has the following text: *The Nigerin Boys.* Text on the under surface of the platform is largely effaced due to flaking of the paint, with only the first word, *BIG*, remaining. We have not been able to identify a Nigerian football team named *Nigerian* or *Nigerin Boys*. Although the word *Nigerin* is probably a misspelling (unintentional or intentional) of *Nigerian* it could conceivably be a reference to Niger, the nation situated at the northern border of Nigeria.

The serpentine appendages on either side of the face mask held mirrors that were attached by nails that remain. The face of the mask has an unusually dolichocephalic form. It is decorated with circular designs on the cheeks created with white and black dots. The number "8" is inscribed with black paint in each of two circles painted with white dots on each cheek that also form the number "8."

Fig. 201

FACE MASK
Anang (Ibibio) People: Nigeria
Materials: *Wood, paint, rubber. H 17.5 in.*

On the superstructure of this mask **(Fig. 202)** there is a kneeling man wearing a red shirt that is decorated with the painted image of a horse or donkey. His arms are outstretched to hold a snake that forms an arch over his head. The snake appears to have grasped the coiffure of the face mask in its mouth. In addition to a single dot on each cheek and a string of fine dots down the middle of its forehead, the face mask has three curved lines that resemble cat whisker at the corners of its mouth. A band of rubber from a bicycle tire inner tube is attached to the back of the mask.

Fig. 202

FACE MASK
Anang (Ibibio) People: Nigeria
Materials: *Wood, paint, rubber. H 15 in.*

The kneeling female figure on the superstructure of this mask **(Fig. 201)** is framed by two snakes that form an arch over her head. She is holding one of the snakes in each of her outstretched hands. The mask's face is decorated with a green forehead dot from which strings of small dots radiate over the forehead, cheeks, and the ridge of the nose. The kneeling female figure and two snakes may be a reference to Mami Wata. A band of rubber from the inner tube of a bicycle tire is attached to the back of the mask.

Fig. 203

FACE MASK
Anang (Ibibio) People: Nigeria
Materials: *Wood, paint, nails, rubber. H 22 in.*

The superstructure of this mask (**Fig. 204**) displays a standing woman dressed in a contemporary belted skirt and short-sleeved blouse with buttons down the front. Each of her hands grasps one of the two snakes whose tails cross at her feet. The face mask is decorated with a forehead dot and a dot on each cheek. The initials *L.T.O.*, possibly identifying the maker of the mask, appear on the front edge of the coiffure. A rubber strap made from a bicycle tire inner tube has been attached to the back of the mask.

Fig. 204

FACE MASK
Anang (Ibibio) People: Nigeria
Materials: *Wood, paint, nails. H 21.5 in.*

The man with parted hair seated astride this face mask (**Fig. 203**) is dressed in a stylish, contemporary outfit. The facial features, white skin tone, and parted hair raise the possibility that the figure represents a European or South American person, possibly a celebrity. His right hand grasps a snake. He is missing the right forearm and hand which probably also grasped a snake. The face mask is decorated with a red forehead dot, dotted designs on the cheeks, and three strands of dots that radiate from each corner of the mouth.

Fig. 205

FACE MASK
Anang (Ibibio) People: Nigeria
Materials: *Wood, paint, nails. H 20 in.*

The female figure seated on top of this mask is wearing a contemporary, short-sleeved dress. Her arms are articulated at the shoulders, and elbows. One of the lateral appendages is missing. The same facial decorations, consisting of single vertical lines on each cheek and three short lines radiating from each corner of the mouth are present on the face of the female figure and the face mask. Both also have similar hairstyles.

The female figure with articulated arms is reminiscent of an Ibibio *Ekon* Society puppet. The *Ekon* Society was an important association of young Ibibio men, who used rod puppets to perform humorous and satirical plays. In addition to being entertaining, the performances were a form of social criticism and control. The arms of the puppets were articulated at the shoulders, and they sometimes had a moveable lower jaw similar to that of the Ogoni mask. *Ekon* Societies have largely been replaced by new forms of entertainment among the Ibibio people, perhaps including figures with articulated arms situated on masks.

147

Fig. 206

FACE MASK
Anang (Ibibio) People: Nigeria
Materials: *Wood, nails. H 18 in.*

The superstructure of this mask is a seated female figure wearing a dress whose arms are articulated at the shoulders and move freely. The parted lips reveal two incisor teeth. The forehead, cheeks and chin of the face mask are decorated with markings that may be based on traditional painted *uli* body art designs that are created with a stain made from the *Uli* plant.

Fig. 207

FACE MASK
Anang (Ibibio) People: Nigeria
Materials: *Wood, paint, nails. H 29 in.*

The elaborate superstructure of this mask **(Fig. 208)**, including a pair of horses, a vertical snake on either side, and an eagle, is derived from the Nigerian coat of arms. The Y-shaped design on the post between the horses represents the confluence of the Niger and Benue Rivers that drain the Western and Eastern parts of Nigeria, respectively. The face mask is decorated with cross hatch designs on the forehead and chin, representing scarifications, as well as a single dot on each cheek.

Fig. 208

FACE MASK
Anang (Ibibio) People: Nigeria
Materials: *Wood, paint, nails, rubber. H 23 in.*

The face of this mask **(Fig. 207)** appears to register surprise at the presence of a scorpion encircled by two snakes on top of its head. The snakes cross behind the scorpion's tail and the head of one of the snakes has been lost. The face of the mask is decorated by three curved lines that radiate from the corners of its mouth. A band of rubber is attached to the back of the mask.

Fig. 209

FACE MASK
Anang (Ibibio) People: Nigeria
Materials: *Wood, paint, nails, rubber. H 19.5 in.*

The superstructure of this mask consists of two horses standing on their hind legs with their forelegs resting on a Y-shaped post that arises from a cap worn by the face mask. The bodies of the horses and the cap are decorated with paired arcs. The heads of the horses are turned to face toward the front of the mask. An eye consisting of the sclera and iris has been painted on the front of the stem of the Y. The arrangement of the horses and Y-shaped post, a reference to the confluence of the Niger and Benue Rivers is probably inspired by the Nigerian coat of arms. The face mask is decorated with dotted designs on each temple, a dotted line on the forehead and nose, and three curled lines radiating from each corner of the mouth. A band of rubber has been attached to the back of the mask.

Fig. 210

FACE MASK

Anang (Ibibio) People: Nigeria
Materials: *Wood, paint, mirrors. H 20.5 in.*

The superstructure of this mask is an eagle standing proudly upright with partly extended wings. The face mask is framed by appendages with mirrors in two of the four circular ends. Decorative designs of black and white dots appear on the cheeks and nose of the face mask and also on the lateral appendages.

The eagle is standing on an arched base, the front of which bears the partly effaced inscription "Made In China" that might refer to tensions caused by the negative economic consequences of cheap Chinese products flooding local Nigerian markets.

Fig. 211

FACE MASK
Anang (Ibibio) People: Nigeria
Materials: *Wood, paint, nails, mirror. H 20 in.*

The superstructure of this nicely painted mask **(Fig. 212)** consists of a snake arched over a bird pecking the head of a second snake. Each of the four circular ends of the appendages on the sides of the mask held mirrors, but only one mirror remains. The face mask has paired linear decorations on the cheeks, central linear decorations on the nose, upper lip and chin, and three curled lines radiating from each corner of the mouth.

Fig. 212

FACE MASK
Anang (Ibibio) People: Nigeria
Materials: *Wood, paint, nails, rubber. H 20.5 in.*

The superstructure of this exquisitely carved and painted mask **(Fig. 211)** consists of an off-white, spotted snake arched over a long-necked red bird that is decorated with black and white spots. The face mask has a red forehead dot, large red dots on the cheeks, and three curved, dotted lines that radiate from the corners of the mouth. A band of rubber has been attached to the back of the mask.

Fig. 213

FACE MASK
Anang (Ibibio) People: Nigeria
Materials: *Wood, paint, nails, yarn, rubber. H 20 in.*

The superstructure of this interesting mask **(Fig. 214)** consists of a bird, possibly a parrot with spread wings, standing upright on a snake coiled at the top of the face mask. A red and white star-shaped object projects from the top of the bird's head. The parrot is sometimes associated with chiefs and diviners because of its ability to "speak." Yarn has been used to create hair on the face mask which reveals prominent teeth through parted lips. There is one small, silver colored ring in each ear lobe. A band of rubber has been attached to the back of the mask.

Fig. 214

FACE MASK
Anang (Ibibio) People: Nigeria
Materials: *Wood, paint. H 12 in.*

The facial features of this mask are similar to those of the preceding mask **(Fig. 213)**, suggesting that it is probably the work of the same carver. There are dots on each cheek and on the forehead. An owl with folded wings and large, dark eyes is perched on top of the mask. A nocturnal hunter endowed with unusually keen eyesight, frontal eyes, and silent flight, the owl has been associated with witchcraft and death. An owl landing in a village at night is said to warn of death to come.

FACE MASK

Anang (Ibibio) People: Nigeria
Materials: *Wood, paint, nails. H 25 in.*

The superstructure of this mask **(Fig. 215)** consists of two snakes arched over a light gray owl with red eyes. The dark gray face mask is decorated with a forehead dot, marks on the cheeks, and three curved lines that radiate from the corners of the mouth.

Fig. 215

Fig. 216

FACE MASK

Anang (Ibibio) People: Nigeria
Materials: *Wood, paint, nails. H 21 in.*

The superstructure of this mask **(Fig. 216)** depicts a kneeling man dressed in military attire. One booted foot rests on a snake as he aims his rifle at an unseen target. The other booted foot is placed against a branching object that might be a tree.

Fig. 217

HEAD CREST MASK (*Zumu*)
Katana (Mama) People: Nigeria
Materials: *Wood, pigment, cloth. H 10 in. W 18 in.*

This mask is an abstract representation of the head of a dwarf forest buffalo that is danced by a member of the *Mangam* Society, a men's association devoted to maintaining social order and encouraging agricultural productivity. The mask is worn horizontally on top of the head. As a wild, unpredictable bush animal, the buffalo is a metaphor for the uncivilized, uncultured, animalistic aspects of human nature. A voluminous raffia costume envelopes the individual who wears the mask.

Fig. 218

Fig. 219

HEAD CREST MASK
Mumuye People: Nigeria
Materials: *Wood, pigment. H 9 in. W 18 in.*

The Mumuye created masks **(Fig. 218)** called *Va* or *Vabou* to represent animals such as the buffalo, monkey, and elephant for use at the end of initiation rites. Initiates were called the "sons of *Va*." These masks also appeared during planting and harvest festivals and at funerals. The mask shown here is thought to depict a buffalo.

HEAD CREST MASK
Mumuye People: Nigeria
Materials: *Wood, pigment. H 9 in. W 13 in.*

This *Va* or *Vabou* mask **(Fig. 219)** of an unidentified animal is similar to the buffalo mask depicted in **Fig. 218**, but it lacks horns.

Fig. 220

SHOULDER MASK
Wurkum People: Nigeria, Chad
Materials: *Wood, metal, pigment. H 29.5 in.*

The Wurkum people who inhabit the Benue River region of northeastern Nigeria and neighboring Chad use a relatively heavy mask associated with fertility. It has been variously reported that these masks were carried on the head or on a shoulder of the dancer. These masks appeared in groups at planting and harvest ceremonies.

The example shown has a dark, granular patina, most evident on the head, ring around the neck, and the upper part of the base that was probably caused by the application of libations. The residue of red pigment is evident in the mouth and in the ears. In addition to metal rings in the ears, hair, and chin the figure has a substantial wooden neck ring that might be a replica of a type of brass currency ring. The mask is carried by a man who is hidden by a straw outfit.

Fig. 221

Fig. 222

Fig. 223

HEAD CREST MASK
Ejagham (Ekoi) People:
Cameroon; Nigeria
Materials: *Wood, metal, pigments, leather, plant fibers. H 11.5 in.*

The human figure with detachable arms and legs seated on this head crest has the characteristics of a puppet, but it is not articulated. The mask attached to a basketry cap is worn on top of the head during *Ekpe* Society performances. It consists of a wood form that is covered with supple animal skin, usually from an antelope, that tightens as it dries.

Fig. 224

HELMET MASK *(Mbap Mgteng)*
Bamileke People: Cameroon
Materials: *Raffia, textile, glass beads, thread. H 59 in.*

This hooded helmet mask is adorned with decorative designs created from glass beads sewn to a raffia textile. Beads are markers of prestige and wealth. These masks are emblematic of the elephant, considered to be a royal animal, and are worn by members of the *Kuosi* Society, originally a warrior group but more recently an association of powerful, wealthy men. They appear at yearly events to celebrate the wealth of the kingdom and members of the Society. The long cloth flaps hanging from the front and back of the mask are covered with beadwork and represent the elephant's trunk. The elephant's ears are depicted by beaded discs on either side of the face. The flaps of the illustrated mask depict three crocodiles just below the face and an inverted double-gong, a symbol of authority. Iron gongs of this sort were played resting on the handle, with the bells turned up, to announce the presence of important people or as a prelude to significant events. The king's gongs had beaded handles. The motif of alternating triangles, *gbatu gbatu*, is associated with royalty and may refer to the spots of a leopard. The regalia includes a cloak of indigo-dyed Bamileke textile fringed with fur, a beaded vest and belt, a fly whisk, and in some instances a headdress encircled by a corona of brightly colored, long feathers.

Fig. 225

HEADDRESS MASK (*Ngoin*)
Western Grasslands People: Cameroon
Materials: *Wood, pigment. H 18.5 in.*

Most masks found in the Western Grasslands kingdoms of Cameroon belong either to secret associations, especially the *Kwifoyn* Society that assists the king or *Fon* in maintaining social and religious order in the community or to important families (lineages), whose masks are controlled by the *Kwifoyn* Society. The symbol of the *Kwifoyn* Society is the double gong depicted on the previously illustrated *Mbap Mgteng* beaded mask. Gongs of various sizes up to 4 feet tall comprise sets that belong to the society in each kingdom.

Masks belonging to *Kwifoyn* or to lineages are worn by men of high social status and wealth, but *Kwifoyn* masks are accorded higher status than those belonging to a lineage. In accord with this distinction, masks of the *Kwifoyn* Society move in a solemn, non-dancing procession, whereas lineage masks dance to the accompaniment of drums, rattles, and a balaphone. The masks have several forms that appear in sequence representing male and female figures as well as animals constituting an assemblage of as many as thirty masks. They are an important part of the funeral of a *Fon* and the annual celebration of the kingdom's prosperity during the dry season. Out of their *in situ* context, it is usually not possible to distinguish between lineage and *Kwifoyn* Society masks on the basis of their appearance alone.

Relatively flat masks, a form described as *Kam*, are worn on top of the head with the face tilted toward the sky, whereas the three-dimensional *Ngoin* mask is perched on top of the wearer's head with the face turned to the front. There are no viewing holes in the eyes, nostrils, or mouth of either type of mask. In both instances, the entire head of the wearer, including his face, is covered with a thin cloth through which he can see. The masker is covered by a loose robe. Prior to their use, the masks are anointed with oil or reddish camwood powder. Remnants of the powder sometimes stain places on the mask that were highlighted with white kaolin pigment.

The male *Ngoin* mask illustrated here has a carved fenestrated hairstyle with the X-design that represents a spider, a symbol of wisdom and prophesy. The teeth and eyes are highlighted with traces of white kaolin pigment, and the inner surfaces of the ears retain red pigment, probably derived from camwood.

Among people of the Western Grasslands, spiders such as the tarantula play an important role in divination because they live on and in the ground. This allows them to serve as a link to the ancestors in their subterranean domain. In this cosmology, frogs and toads are symbols of fertility, the ram is associated with important palace officials, and the buffalo refers to royal servants of the king.

Fig. 226

HEAD CREST MASK (*Nkang*)
Western Grasslands People: Cameroon
Materials: *Wood, pigment. H 18 in.*

Nkang masks are part of the repertoire of masks controlled by the *Kwifoyn* Society. They appear at the funerals of society members, celebrations of titleholders, and at an annual dance at the conclusion of the main harvest.

This relatively flat mask of the *kam* type is worn on top of the head. It has the beard and bi-lobed hairstyle with striations running from front to back of a male leader of a lineage mask group. The leader mask is at the head of the procession of lineage or *Kwifoyn* Society masks as they enter and leave the performance area. The figure wears a special outfit and carries staffs that are emblems of male power and authority. Traces of pigment that was used to highlight sculptural features remain around the eyes, in the ears, and in striations carved in the hair and beard.

Fig. 227

HEAD CREST MASK (*Nkang*)
Western Grasslands People: Cameroon
Materials: *Wood, metal, beads. H 16 in.*

The face of this mask is sheathed in thin sheets of brass. The surface of the metal appliqué is enhanced by an embossed design that is best appreciated on the forehead.

The crescent-shaped prestige cap is decorated with appliquéd, small, predominantly white beads arranged in a swirling design, and similar beads appear on the eyes, wings of the nose and beard. This type of cap indicates high status in the royal entourage and is only worn by kings, princes, and important court retainers. The use of beads and brass sheathing, materials reserved for royalty, underscores the high status of this mask.

HEAD CREST MASK *(Tsesah)*
Bamileke People: Cameroon
Materials: *Wood, pigment.*
H 36.5 in.

This very large mask, an abstract depiction of a face, is sometimes referred to as *Batcham* for the kingdom where the earliest examples in Western collections were found in 1904. However, these masks have also been linked to other central Bamileke kingdoms, such as Bamenda and Bandjoun, where evidence suggests they were carved.

The mask belongs to the *Msop* Society. It appears at the installation of a king and at the funerals of kings and other community leaders. In the *tsodung* or elephant dance, the mask celebrates the power of the kingdom. It has been suggested that the mask resembles a hippopotamus, an animal sacred to *Msop*, as it emerges from the water.

The *tsesah* mask is dominated by a vertical, arched element decorated with linear carved designs, possibly a reference to body scarifications. The upper part of the face features prominent almond-shaped eyes situated above bulging cheeks. The lower part of the face consists of a broad wide-open mouth in which teeth are represented by vertical striations. A hollow neck pierced with holes for attaching a costume forms a ring below the mouth.

Fig. 228

Fig. 229

163

Okuy Face Masks of the Punu People in Gabon

The *Okuy* Society mask is an idealized portrait of a deceased female ancestor representing a female guardian spirit who returns for a ceremony, such as a funeral. The white kaolin paint used on the face of most of these masks is a reference to the ancestors and their spirits. Masks with a black, yellow, or red face are uncommon. The masks are embellished with raised carved stylized representations of female scarifications on the forehead and temples. The scarifications usually consist of nine bumps arranged in a diamond configuration on the forehead and a rectangle on each of the temples. Rarely, more than nine bumps are present. Eyes reduced to narrow slightly arched slits between full upper and lower lids that impart an Oriental expression are a characteristic feature of the *Okuy* mask. The elaborate coiffure is typically divided into three sections with a dominant central lobe, although other hairstyles are sometimes present. *Okuy* maskers, clothed in raffia or cloth outfits, perform acrobatic dances on stilts at funerals, at the initiation of young girls, to celebrate ancestors, and at new moon festivals. They are accompanied by assistants who protect them by keeping onlookers at bay.

Fig. 230

Fig. 231

FACE MASK *(Okuy)*
Punu People: Gabon
Materials: *Wood, pigment.*
H *12 in.*

This white-faced mask demonstrates many of the characteristic features found in *Okuy* masks. The 9 globular red forehead scarifications on this white-faced mask form a diamond, whereas the 9 scarifications on the temples form vertically oriented rectangles. A slender rounded ridge runs along the crest of the large central hair lobe that thrusts forward over the forehead. Carved striations on the surfaces of the hair lobes indicate the direction in which the hair has been combed. Triangular, non-striated objects on the lateral hair lobes represent combs used to hold the hair in place.

Fig. 232

Fig. 233

FACE MASK *(Okuy)*
Punu People: Gabon
Materials: *Wood, pigment. H 9 in.*

There is a cleft in the upper part of the central relatively low hair lobe of this white-faced mask **(Fig. 232)**. The semilunar area without striations at the front of the central hair lobe may represent a comb with a function similar to that of the combs on the lateral hair lobes.

FACE MASK *(Okuy)*
Punu People: Gabon
Materials: *Wood, pigment. H 9 in.*

The surface of the tower hairstyle on this mask **(Fig. 233)** is smooth. The forehead is colored orange, and the face is white. Scarifications are absent from the forehead and temples.

Fig. 234

FACE MASK (*Okuy*)
Punu People: Gabon
Materials: *Wood, pigment.*
H 12.5 in.

This dark brown mask has the tower hairstyle. Traces of hair that was pasted to the surface are palpable. There are no scarifications on the forehead or temples. Thin lines that extend laterally from the nasal alae across the cheeks represent an ornamental wire that was passed through the nose in this position. Black and brown *Okuy* masks with features similar to white masks were worn by judges seeking witches and criminals.

FACE MASK (*Okuy*)
Punu People: Gabon
Materials: *Wood, pigment, brass, cloth. H 8.5 in.*

This black mask **(Fig. 235)** has a relatively small central hair lobe with a braided band running along the crest. Small cloth packages that may contain "medicine" are situated at the base of the central hair lobe and at the tip of the chin. A small brass plate embedded in the forehead might be a substitute for the usual carved scarifications, and the white rectangles on the temples may have the same purpose.

Fig. 235

Fig. 236

FACE MASK (*Okuy*)
Punu People: Gabon
Materials: *Wood, pigment. H 12.5 in.*

Only a small percentage of *Okuy* masks have the yellow or ochre face displayed by this example **(Fig. 236)** with a large, forward-protruding, central hair lobe. This mask has the typical diamond shaped cluster of nine scarifications on the forehead. The temporal elements are two parallel raised zigzag bands comprising a total of six scarifications on each side of the face.

Fig. 237

Fig. 238

FACE MASK (*Okuy*)
Punu People: Gabon
Materials: *Wood, pigment.*
H 15.5 in.

Okuy masks with an animal figure on the crown, such as this white-faced example, are rare. The bird is situated in a cleft in the center of the coiffure that is defined by a broad crosshatched design rather than the close striations seen in most *Okuy* masks. Typical frontal and temporal scarifications are present. The identity of the bird is uncertain, but the large beak raises the possibility that it could be a hornbill bird.

FACE MASK (*Ekuk*)
Kwele People: Gabon
Materials: *Wood, pigment. H 15.5 in.*

Kwele masks **(Fig. 239)** with a heart-shaped face are used by the *Bwete* Society to maintain social order by drawing upon the powers of ancestors to resolve disputes and deal with threats to the community, such as epidemics and natural disasters. The masks are thought to represent forest spirits embodied by the term *ekuk*, meaning "things of the forest." They appear during initiation, mourning ceremonies, and at times of crisis in several forms made of wood or fiber.

This *ekuk* mask has a central heart-shaped, slightly concave face with a triangular nose, and narrow eyes. Arches that resemble horns arise from the crown of the head and curve around the face. Secondary faces may be found on the arches. The white kaolin pigment used to paint the masks represents light and clairvoyance, attributes necessary to combat evil spirits. The dancer wears a costume composed of raffia and animal fur with painted body markings and ankle rattles.

Fig. 239

Fig. 240

FACE MASK (*Booag*)
Kwele People: Gabon
Materials: *Wood, pigments. H 21 in.*

This variant of an *ekuk* mask **(Fig. 240)** belonging to the *Bwete* Society appears during ceremonies devoted to countering the negative effects of witchcraft during periods of communal crisis. It is an abstract depiction of the head of a bongo antelope. The tips of the horns have been damaged.

FACE MASK
Kwele People: Gabon
Materials: *Wood, pigments. H 13 in.*

The face of this uncommon Kwele mask **(Fig. 241)** features three pairs of eyes with only the central pair perforated.

Fig. 241

Fig. 242

FACE MASK (*Ngil*)
Fang People: Gabon; Equatorial Guinea; Cameroon
Materials: *Wood, pigment. H 28 in.*

These masks **(Fig. 242)** are worn by members of the *Ngil* Society. They are characterized by a calm, solemn, elongated face with minimal representation of the eyes and mouth. The faces of these masks are usually painted with white kaolin clay to embody the spirits of ancestors. Illuminated by torchlight, the maskers appear during nocturnal initiation ceremonies or to punish witches and criminals.

Fig. 243

FACE MASK (*Kpongadomba*)
Boa People: Democratic Republic Of Congo
Materials: *Wood, pigment. H 12 in.*

The Boa people are farmers and hunters. It has been suggested that the prominent ears of this mask **(Fig. 244)** refer to the keen sense of hearing needed to be a successful hunter and warrior. It is also possible that the mask depicts the enlarged ears of the Boa people created by inserting wood or ivory discs into their ear lobes. Contrasting pigments such as black and white often define geometric areas on the surface of Boa masks. The uses of these masks are obscure. Some authors have identified them as war masks. Recent studies suggest that they were used for initiation ceremonies.

Fig. 244

FACE MASK (*Ngil*)
Fang People: Gabon;
Equatorial Guinea; Cameroon
Materials: *Wood, pigment.*
H 16.5 in.

In contrast to the preceding, relatively abstract example, facial features of this *Ngil* mask **(Fig. 243)** are more clearly defined because the hair and nose are colored brown. Scarification can be seen on one cheek.

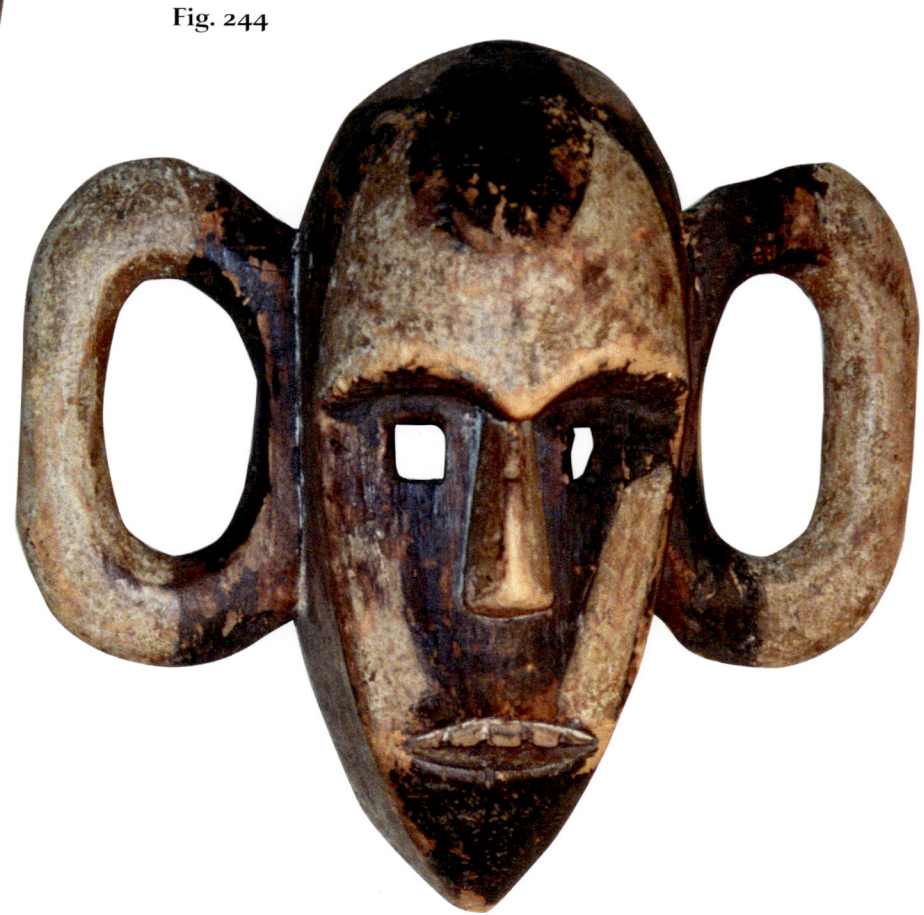

Fig. 245

FACE MASK (*Mwisi Gwa So'o*)
Hemba People: Democratic Republic Of Congo
Materials: *Wood, pigment. H 7 in.*

This mask with simian features is thought to represent the spirit of a chimpanzee. It is characterized by a prominent, open mouth, elevated eyebrows, and large eyelids that constitute a socially unacceptable facial expression for the Hemba people. These features are the antithesis of the calm, reserved demeanor and closed mouth considered to be the Hemba ideal. The costume includes a wig and beard of black and white monkey fur. The performer also wears furs from domestic and wild animals and bark cloth. The *So'o* mask appears at second funeral rites in a performance that combines aggressive behavior with amusing pantomime of actions not ordinarily considered to be topics for public discussion. The dance assists in the transition between the trauma caused by a death and the return to a more normal state of affairs after the departure of the deceased to the land of the ancestors.

Kifwebe Face Masks of the Songye People, Democratic Republic of Congo

Belonging to the men's *Bwadi* Society, *kifwebe* masks were traditionally danced at funerals, initiation and healing ceremonies, or to intimidate an enemy. More recently the masks have appeared mostly for entertainment. Members of the society are believed to be imbued with supernatural powers to influence the actions of spirits. Male masks *(kilume)* have a saggital crest on the top of the head that is lacking from female masks *(kikashi)*. The linear channeled design on the head and neck of the mask is often painted white (peace and purity), black (dark magic or evil), or black and white. Red (courage, blood or danger) may also be used. Female masks are typically white and have finely carved channels. Male masks, usually black, red, as well as white, have broader channels. Small tufts of plant fibers or hair may protrude from holes in the lower surface of the nose, but this material often deteriorates and is lost as a result of use and age. The masquerade includes a costume of tightly fitting woven netting, gloves, and a raffia beard.

Fig. 246

FACE MASK (*Kifwebe*)
Songye People: Democratic Republic Of Congo
Materials: *Wood, pigment.*
H 20 in.

This white-faced, female *kifwebe* mask has finely carved channels arranged in four distinct patterns that correspond to and accentuate different planes of the surface. The eyes, nose, and mouth are highlighted in black.

Fig. 247

Fig. 248

FACE MASK (*Kifwebe*)
Songye People:
Democratic Republic Of Congo
Materials: *Wood, pigment. H 22 in.*

This male mask has a modest crest, a triangular protruding nose, and a long jutting rectangular mouth. The semi-lunar bulging upper eyelids are painted red. The channels carved in this male mask are deeper and broader than those in the typical female mask, and they extend over the surfaces of the crest, nose, and mouth. The lateral view reveals smooth transitions in the direction of the channels as they flow over different surfaces of the mask. Much of the pigment has been lost from channels that were red, white, and black in alternating sets of two or three of the same color.

Fig. 249

FACE MASK *(Kifwebe)*
Songye People:
Democratic Republic Of Congo
Materials: *Wood, pigment. H 18 in.*

This male mask is dominated by a large forward-protruding crest that ends at the apex of the triangular nose. The rectangular mouth juts forward beneath the nose. Very broad channels are distributed in a harmonious pattern that follows the contour of the crest and flows around the slit-shaped eyes with black bulging upper and lower lids. Alternate channels are painted black and white.

Fig. 250

Fig. 251

HEADDRESS MASK
Budja People: Democratic Republic Of Congo
Materials: *Wood, plant fibers, Abrus precatorius seeds, pigment. H 19 in.*

The Budja people are primarily farmers living near the Lualaba River in the north of the Democratic Republic of Congo. The mask is thought to be the abstract representation of a mythical animal with features of an antelope and a bird. It is attached to a basket woven from plant fibers that is worn on the top of the head when it appears at festivals related to farming and hunting.

Fig. 252

FACE MASK
Lwalwa People:
Democratic Republic
Of Congo; Angola
Materials: *Wood, pigment. H 12 in.*

Masks of the Lwalwa people have distinctive geometric planes that are represented by rectangular eyes and a prominent nose reminiscent of a bird's beak. These masks were traditionally used in the initiation rites of the men's secret *Ngongo* Society and in rites to appease spirits involved with hunting, but they now appear at various public celebrations. Worn exclusively by men, the masks appear in pairs representing male *(nkaki)* and female *(cifola)* figures, respectively. The nose of the male mask juts further forward from the plane of the face and at a more acute angle than the nose of the female mask. The nose of a male mask does not have the sharp edge found on a female mask, such as the example that is illustrated here. White kaolin pigment highlights the eyes and mouth. Just above the mouth is a hole through which a knotted cord was passed to be held in the dancer's teeth. The face of the mask has been painted with a red plant juice. The cap-like carving on top of the head represents the coiffure.

Face Masks of the Chokwe People Democratic Republic of Congo and Angola

The Chokwe people have masculine *(chihongo)* and feminine *(mwanapwo)* masks. Both types bear distinct carved designs on the forehead, cheeks, and chin. Masculine masks that depict a wealthy, noble, or elder man have a discoid protrusion representing a beard below the chin. They are associated with judiciary and tax collecting functions. Feminine masks tend to be finely carved with a serene appearance. They represent a female ancestor and the ideal of youthful feminine beauty.

Because of its ability to grow continuously, hair is considered to have attributes that relate to an individual's life force. As a consequence, hair has powerful properties that extend to the simulated hair, usually made from plant material that is attached to Chokwe masks as well as to beads and other decorative material used to adorn the coiffure of a mask. Hair from another person can be used to inflict harm on that individual. Any strand of hair or decorative material that is detached during a performance must be promptly retrieved so that is does not fall into someone else's hands. Hair is sometimes enclosed in amulets for protection against witchcraft.

A cross-shaped scarification on the forehead *(chingeleyele)* is based on the Maltese cross, a symbol found on a type of tin pendant brought by the Portuguese who colonized Angola. These pendants served as amulets among the Chokwe people and were attached to their hair or worn as earrings. Various other finely carved facial scarifications include a motif of paired tears below the eyes *(masoji)*, paired chevrons on the cheeks *(tukone)*, paired horizontal lines on the temples *(mipila)*, and a vertical mark on the forehead and nose *(kangongo)*. White kaolin pigment is sometimes used to highlight the teeth and interior of the ears. A woven net made from plant fibers secures the mask on the wearer's head. The remainder of the costume is also composed of tightly woven plant fibers colored with red, white, and black striped designs. Wooden breasts are attached to the chest of an outfit that represents a female figure. A strip of cloth that may be decorated with beads, coins, and other items can be found at the junction of the face and the coiffure. It corresponds to a type of headband worn by the Chokwe.

Fig. 253

FACE MASK (*Chihongo*)
Chokwe People: Democratic Republic Of Congo
Materials: *Wood, plant fibers, pigment. H 10 in.*

This male mask exhibits a discoid protrusion representing a beard below the chin. It has the *chingeleyele* Maltese cross and *masoji* teardrop scarifications carved as raised designs, respectively, on the forehead and below the eyes.

181

FACE MASK (*Mwanapwo*)
Chokwe People: Democratic Republic of Congo; Angola
Materials: *Wood, pigment, plant fibers. H 9 in.*

The only facial scarifications on this female mask are three, evenly spaced, short, parallel lines at the corners of the mouth. The whitened teeth have been chiseled to points, duplicating a past practice of the Chokwe people. Netting, used to hold traditional coiffure, is indicated by a carved pattern on the head.

Fig. 254

FACE MASK (*Mwanapwo*)
Chokwe People: Democratic Republic Of Congo; Angola
Materials: *Wood, plant fibers, pigment. H 8.5 in.*

This female mask has the Maltese cross forehead marking (*chingeleyele*) as well as scarifications on the cheeks and chin, all indicated by incised designs. Teeth chiseled to points and the inner surfaces of the ears are highlighted with white pigment.

Fig. 255

FACE MASK (*Mwanapwo*)
Chokwe People: Democratic Republic Of Congo; Angola
Materials: *Wood cloth, pigment. H 9 in.*

The only scarification on the face of this female mask is the elevated *chingeleyele* cross on the forehead. The facial features are finely carved, including full lips parted to reveal chiseled teeth. The crosshatched incised design on top of the mask represents netting that was used to hold coiffure in place. A remnant of the red cloth that covered the head of the masker is attached to the back of the mask.

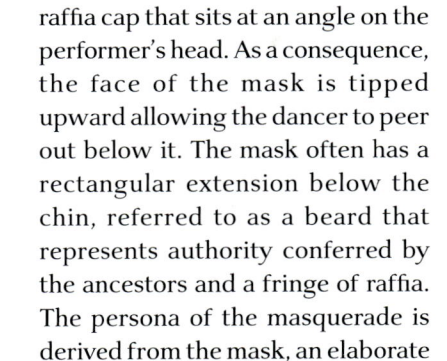

Fig. 256

FACE MASK (*Mbuya Or Muyombo*)
Pende People: Democratic Republic Of Congo
Materials: *Wood, raffia, pigment. H 7.5 in.*

This mask is attached to a woven raffia cap that sits at an angle on the performer's head. As a consequence, the face of the mask is tipped upward allowing the dancer to peer out below it. The mask often has a rectangular extension below the chin, referred to as a beard that represents authority conferred by the ancestors and a fringe of raffia. The persona of the masquerade is derived from the mask, an elaborate costume of cloth, raffia, feathers, leaves, and other materials all forming part of the choreography of the dance. Shaking a rattle, the dancer moves with a distinctive shuffling walk and is heard before being seen. The performances have various subjects, including the celebration of women's work related to food production such as cooking, hoeing, and fishing, or they may offer satirical commentary on customs and values of the Pende people.

Fig. 257

HELMET MASK (Kipoko)
Pende People: Democratic Republic Of Congo
Materials: *Wood, pigment. H 10 in.*

Kipoko, a chief's mask of the eastern Pende people, performs a dance using one or two flywhisks as props as a celebration of thanksgiving for the harvests and children born in the previous year. Movements incorporated in the dance include flicking of the flywhisk to mimic the agricultural and domestic activities of men and women that sustain the community. Flicking the ground with the flywhisk is a gesture to ensure a healthy village by sweeping away evil spirits. The dancer also makes energetic, semicircular kicks over medicine buried in the dance arena or over persons in need to implore ancestors for protection from malevolent agents that attack individuals or the community. The dancer may also mimic many daily communal activities involved with the production of food such as hunting, drawing palm wine, or hoeing. *Kipoko* masks also appear during the initiation rite for boys.

As the embodiment of the power of the ancestors and the authority of the chief, the *kipoko* mask is kept in the chief's home. The form of the mask with a long nose is a reference to the vigilance that requires a chief to use his sense of smell to detect the odor of evil. The large eyes and protruding ears, as well as the prominent nose, indicate the chief's attention to what is going on in his village. The mask's small mouth denotes the importance of speaking judiciously and only when necessary. The shelf-like projection at the lower edge of the mask may represent a beard as a symbol of wisdom. Because of its importance to the chief, the *Kipoko* mask is carefully maintained by being repainted and repaired when cracks or holes develop as a result of repeated use. The illustrated *Kipoko* mask has a repaired hole on one side of the face.

Fig. 258

Fig. 259

Fig. 260

FACE MASK (*?Pumbu*)
Pende People:
Democratic Republic of Congo
Materials: *Wood, pigment. H 23.5 in.*

The *pumbu* mask with its hollow, cylindrical form is one of several objects associated with royal authority, including the *Kipoko* mask that are kept in a chief's ritual house. *Pumbu*, the most powerful of the masks, appears on rare occasions when the community is seriously endangered, such as a famine or when the chief is seriously ill. The masked figure carries a weapon and is restrained by attendants holding ropes attached to his waist during his threatening dance that symbolizes the power and courage of the chief as he confronts a threat to the community.

The mask illustrated here has the hollow cylindrical form with a domed top, elongated nose, and bands of black and white triangles that characterize a *pumbu* mask. However, it differs from published examples that have tubular eyes, a small open rectangular mouth displaying sharp teeth, and a knob on the crown of the head.

Fig. 261   Fig. 262

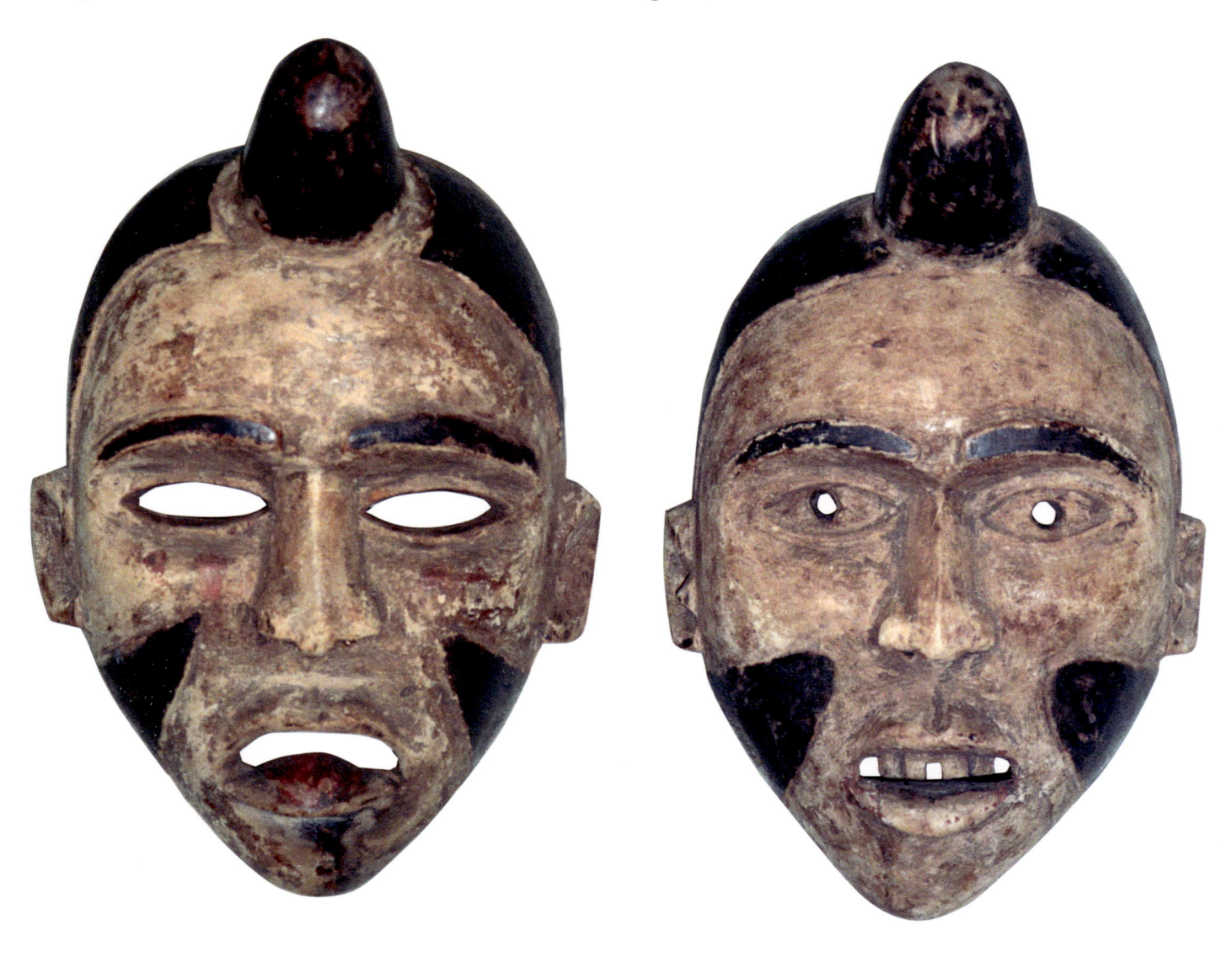

FACE MASKS (*Nganga Di Phombe*)
Yombe People: Democratic Republic Of Congo
Materials: *Wood, pigment.* Fig. 261: *H 13.5 in.*; Fig. 262: *H 13.5 in.*

The Yombe people are one of several tribes who comprised the original Kongo kingdom in the 13th–16th centuries. The homeland of the Yombe is the western part of what is now the Democratic Republic of Congo. Yombe masks tend to have a naturalistic face with white coloration that is a reference to the spirit world as well as to clairvoyance, truth, and justice. Black, triangular areas on the cheeks may be abstract representations of scarifications. The knob on top of the head refers to a peaked hairstyle worn by Kongo women of high status.

These masks were worn by a ritual diviner, the *nganga di phombe*, who was able to find witchcraft, reveal the causes of social disharmony or explain a natural disaster by identifying an individual who was the cause of the problem.

HELMET MASK (*Bwoom*)
Kuba People: Democratic Republic Of Congo
Materials: *Wood, copper, fibers, hide, cowrie shell, seeds, cloth, glass beads. H 23 in.*

Bwoom, one of the three central figures cited in Kuba mythology, is represented by this impressive helmet mask with a bulging forehead. The prominent forehead is thought to be a caricature of the physiognomy of Twa, a pygmy. Sheets of copper, beads, and cowrie shells used to decorate the mask were signs of wealth, authority, and leadership used only by court artists. Bwoom plays multiple roles including that of a commoner, a pygmy, or the brother of the king. Woot, the king, appears as another mask, *mwaash a Mbooy*. The third figure, the king's sister and wife, is represented by the *ngady a Mwash* mask. Masks representing these characters belong to the king and can only be danced with his permission. Lacking eyeholes, the Bwoom mask is placed on top of the head at an angle so that the performer can see through the nostrils. The flap hanging in front serves to disguise the wearer's face. Bwoom appears at various events including initiation rites.

Fig. 265

Fig. 264

Fig. 263

187

Fig. 266

FACE MASK *(Ndunga)*
Woyo People: Democratic Republic Of Congo
Materials: *Wood, paint, brass tacks. H 17 in.*

The Woyo are a subgroup of the Kongo people who live in a region bordered by the Atlantic Ocean and the Zaire river near Angola. They are known for their relatively large polychrome masks that sometimes have geometric areas painted in different colors. Dots of color are thought to represent the spots of a leopard, tears, or smallpox lesions. In this instance, brass tacks have been used to enhance the power and visibility of the mask. The very bulky costume of banana leaves and mask are called ndunga, meaning to be hidden and enormous. Ndunga participates in religious ceremonies, funerals of important persons, and the installation of a chief.

References

Adams, S. "Praise Her Beauty Well. Ùrì from the Body to Cloth." In *Call and Response*. S. Adams, L. Williams, B. Martinez-Ruiz (eds). Yale University Art Gallery, New Haven, 2000, pp. 9-45.

Bach, S., and W. Siegmann. *Assuming the Guise. African Masks Considered and Reconsidered*. Williams College Museum of Art, Williamstown, 1991.

Baquart, J-B. *The Tribal Arts of Africa*. Thames and Hudson, New York, 1998.

Bentor, E. "Spatial Continuities. Masks and Cultural Interactions Between the Delta and Southeastern Nigeria." *African Arts* 2002; 35: 26-41,93.

Berns, M.C., and R. Fardon. "Central Nigeria Unmasked: Arts of the Benue River Valley." *African Arts* 2011; 44: 16-37.

Berzock, K.B., and C. Clarke (eds). *Representing Africa in American Art Museums: A Century of Collecting and Display*. University of Washington Press, Seattle, 2011.

Biebuyck, D. "Introduction" in *Tradition and Creativity in Tribal Art*, D. Biebuyck (ed). University of California Press, Berkeley, 1969, pp. 1-23.

Biloti, A., G. Calme-Griaule, and F. N'Diaye. *Masques du Pays Dogon*. Adam Biro, Paris, 2001.

Bleakley, R. *African Masks*. St. Martin's Press, New York, 1978.

Boone, S.A. *Radiance From the Waters. Ideals of Feminine Beauty in Mende Art*. Yale University Press, New Haven, 1986.

Carey, N. *Masks of the Koranko Poro. Form, Function and Comparison to the Toma*. Ethnos Publications, Amherst, 2007.

Celenko, T. *A Treasury of African Art from the Harrison Eiteljorg Collection*. Indiana University Press, Bloomington, 1983.

Ceyssens, R. "The 'Bwa War Masks' of the Middle Uele Region." *African Arts* 2007: 40: 8-73.

Cohen, P. "Federal Inquiry Into Artworks Possibly Forged." *The New York Times*, Saturday, December 3, 2001.

Cole, H.M., and C.C. Aniakor. *Igbo Arts: Community and Cosmos*. University of California, Los Angeles, Los Angeles, 1984.

Cole, H.M. (ed). *I Am Not Myself: The Art of African Masquerade*. University of California Los Angeles, Los Angeles, 1985.

Congdon-Martin, D.L., and J. Pieper. *Masks of the World*. Schiffer Publishing Ltd, Atglen, PA, 1999.

Cooksey, S.E. "Plank Mask: Kab (Bush Buffalo)." In *Resonance from the Past: African Sculpture from the New Orleans Museum of Art*. F. Herreman (ed) Cat 7, Museum for African Art, New York, 2005 (pp.22-23).

Cotter, H. "Under Threat: The Shock of the Old." *The New York Times*, Art and Leisure Section, April 11, 2011.

Drewal, H.J., J. Pemberton III, and R. Abiodun. *Yoruba. Nine Centuries of African Art and Thought*. The Center for African Art and Harry N Abrams, New York, 1995.

Drewal, H.J. "Sources and Currents." In *Mami Wata: Arts for Water Spirits in Africa and Its Diasporas*. H.J. Drewal (ed). Fowler Museum at the UCLA, Los Angeles, 2008.

Duquette, D.G. "Women, Power, and Initiation in the Bissagos Islands." *African Arts*, 1979: 31-34, 1993.

_____. *Dynamique de l'Art Bidjogo*. Instituto de Investigação Científica Tropical. Lisbon, 1983.

Erdman, S. *Nine Hills to Nambonkaha*. Henry Holt Co., New York, 2003.

Fagg, W., and H. List. *Nigerian Images. The Splendor of African Sculpture*. Alfred A. Praeger, New York, 1963.

Fagg, W. *African Tribal Images. The Katherine Reswick Collection.* The Cleveland Museum of Art, Cleveland, 1968.

———. "The African Artist in Tradition and Creativity." In *Tribal Art.* D. Biebuyck (ed). University of California Press, Berkeley, 1969, pp. 42-57.

Fermé, M.C. *The Underneath of Things. Violence, History and the Everday in Sierra Leone.* University of California Press, Los Angeles, 2001.

Finley, C. *The Art of African Masks: Exploring Cultural Traditions.* Lerner Publishing Group, Minneapolis, 2008.

Galembo, P. *Maske.* Chris Boot Ltd., London, 2010.

Geary, C.M. *Visions of Africa: Bamum.* 5 Continents Editions, Milan, 2011.

Guillaume, P., and T. Munro. *Primitive Negro Sculpture.* Jonathan Cope, London, 1926.

Hahner-Herzog, I., M. Kecskési, and L. Vajda. *African Masks from the Barbier-Mueller Collection, Geneva.* Prestel Verlag, Munich, 1998.

Hart, W.A. "AronArabai: The Temne Mask of Chieftancy." *African Arts* 1986: 19: 41-45, 91.

———. "Limba Funeral Masks." *African Arts* 1988; 22: 60-67, 99.

Herold, E. *The Art of Africa: Tribal Masks From the Nàprstek Museum, Prague.* Paul Hamlyn, London, 1967.

Herreman, F. *Resonance from the Past: African Sculpture from the New Orleans Museum of Art.* Museum for African Art, New York, 2005.

Hinkley, P. *The Sowo Mask: Symbol of Sisterhood.* Working Paper #40 The African Studies Center, Boston University, Boston 1980.

Hommel, W.T. *Art of the Mende.* University of Maryland, College Park, 1974.

Jones, G.I. *The Art of Eastern Nigeria.* Cambridge University Press, New York, 1984.

———. *Ibo Art.* Shire Publications Ltd, Aylesbury, 1989.

Kerchache, J., J-L Paudrat, and L. Stéphan. *Art of Africa.* Harry N. Abrams, New York, 1993.

Lamp, F. *African Art of the West African Coast: Transition in Form and Content.* L. Kahan Gallery, New York, 1979.

———. *Art of the Baga. A Drama of Cultural Reinvention.* Prestel Verlag, Munich, 1996.

Mack, J. "African Masking" in *Masks and the Art of Expression,* J. Mack (ed). Harry N. Abrams, New York, 1994.

Massa, G. *Masques Animaux D'Afrique de L'Ouest.* Editions Sepia-Societé des Amateurs de L'Art Africaine, Paris, 1995.

Mato, D., and C. Miller III. *Sande Masks and Statues from Liberia-Sierra Leone.* Galerie Balolu, Amsterdam, 1990.

McCluskey, P. *Art From Africa. Long Steps Never Broke a Back.* Princeton University Press and Seattle Art Museum, Seattle, 2002.

Meneghini, M. *Collecting African Art in Liberia and Neighboring Countries: 1963-1989.* Nicolini Editore, Italy, 2006.

Messenger, J.C. "The Carver in Anang Society." In *The Traditional Artist in African Societies.* W.L. d'Azevedo (ed). Indiana University Press, Bloomington, 1971, pp 101-127.

Monti, F. *African Masks.* Paul Hamlyn, London, 1969.

Mulinda, H.B. "Masks as Proverbial Language (Woyo, Zaire)." In *Objects. Signs of Africa,* L. deHeusch (ed). Snoeck-Ducaju & Zoon, Ghent, 1995.

Ndiaye, F., and G. Massa. *L'Oisseau dans L'Art de L'Afrique de L'Ouest.* Editions Sepia-Societé des Amateurs de L'Art Africaine, Paris, 2004.

Northern, T. *The Art of Cameroon.* National Museum of Natural History, Smithsonian Institution, Washington 1984.

———. *Expressions of Cameroon Art. The Franklin Collection.* Los Angeles County Museum of Natural History, Los Angeles, 1986.

Nossiter, A. "Police Kill Demonstrators in Major City of Ivory Coast." *The New York Times,* March 9. 2011.

Nunley, J.W. "The Fancy and the Fierce." *African Arts* 1981; 14:52-58, 87-88.

———. *Moving with the Face of the Devil. Art and Politics in Urban West Africa.* University of Illinois Press, Urbana, 1987.

———. "Jolly Masquerades and Mami Wata in Sierra Leone" in *Mami Wata: Arts for Water Spirits in African and Its Diasporas,* H.J. Drewal (ed). Fowler Museum at UCLA, Los Angeles, 2008.

———. Personal Communication, 2011.

Okeke-Agulu, C. "The Persistence of Memory." In *Maske,* P. Galembo (ed). Chris Boot LTD, London, 2010.

Page, D. *A Cameroon World. Art and Artifacts from the Marshall and Caroline Mount Collection.* Queens Community College Art Gallery Press, New York, 2007.

Paulme, D. *African Sculpture.* Viking Press, New York, 1962.

Perrois, L. *Art Ancestral du Gabon.* Musèe Barbier–Mueller, Geneva, 1985.

Petridis, C. *South of the Sahara.* The Cleveland Museum of Art, Cleveland, 2003.

Phillips, R.B. *Representing Women. Sande Masquerades of the Mende of Sierra Leone.* University of California Los Angeles 1995.

Phillips, T. *Africa. Art of a Continent.* Prestel Verlag, Munich, 1997.

Richards, J.V.O. "Santigie Sesay: Sierra Leone Carver." *African Arts* 1977; 11:65-69,92.

Robbins, W.M., and N.I. Nooter. *African Art in American Collections.* Schiffer Publishing, Atglen, PA, 2004.

Roberts, A.F. *Animals in African Art: From the Familiar to the Marvelous.* Prestel Verlag, Munich, 1997.

Rosen, M.S., and P.P. Rosen. *The Colorful Sogo Bò Puppets of Mali*. Schiffer Publishing, Atglen, 2012.

Roy, C.D. *The Art of Burkina Faso. Art and Life in Africa Project*. University of Iowa. http://www.uiowa.edu/~africart

____. *Signs and Symbols in African Art: Graphic Patterns in Burkina Faso. Art and Life in Africa Project*. University of Iowa. http://www.uiowa.edu/~africart

Salmons, J. "Siren Seductress of the Seven Seas: Mami Wata in the Global Village." In *Re-visions: A new perspective on the African Collections of the Horniman Museum,* K Arnaut (ed). Horniman Museum and Gardens, London, 2000.

Scheinberg, A.L., J. Elbers. *Ekon Society Puppets: Sculptures for Social Criticism*. Tribal Arts Gallery, New York, 1977.

Segy, L. *Masks of Black Africa*. Dover Publications, New York, 1976.

Sieber, R., and F. Herreman. *Hair in African Art and Culture*. Prestel Verlag, Munich, 2000.

Siegmann, W., and J. Perani. "Men's Masquerades of Sierra Leone and Liberia." *African Arts,* 1976; 9: 42-47, 92.

Stepan, P. *World Art: Africa*. Prestel Verlag, Munich, 2001.

____. *Spirits Speak. A Celebration of African Masks*. Prestel Verlag, Munich, 2005.

Strother, Z.S. *Inventing Masks. Agency and the Art of the Central Pende*. University of Chicago Press, Chicago, 1988.

Szalay, M (ed). *African Art from the Han Coray Collection 1916-1928*. Prestel Verlag, Munich, 1998.

Teuten, T. *A Collector's Guide to Masks*. Wellfleet Books, Secaucus, 1990.

Van Damme, W. *A Comparative Analysis Concerning Beauty and Ugliness in Sub-Saharan Africa*. Africana Candensia v.4. Rijksuniversiteit, Ghent, 1987.

Visona, M.B., R. Poyner, H.M. Cole, and M.D. Harris. *A History of Art in Africa*. Harry N. Abrams Inc, New York, 2001.

Vogel, S. (ed). *For Spirits and Kings. African Art from the Paul and Ruth Tishman Collection*. Metropolitan Museum of Art, New York, 1981.

Warner, E. *New Song in a Strange Land*. Houghton Mifflin, New York, 1948.

Williams, L. Traveling Concepts: Making and Remaking Culture. In *Call and Response: Journeys of African Art*. S. Adams, L. Williams, B. Martinez-Ruiz (eds). Yale University Art Gallery, New Haven, 2000, pp. 55-78.

Willett F. *African Art: An Introduction, Revised Edition*. Thames and Hudson, New York, 1993

Index of Masks

Country and People	Figure Numbers
ANGOLA	
Lwalwa	252
Chokwe	254-256
BURKINA FASO	
Bobo	142-144
Bwa	135, 141
Marka	127
Mossi	132-134
Nuna or Winiama	140
Nunuma	136, 137
Tusyan or Siemu	130, 131
Winiama	138, 139
CAMEROON	
Bamileke	224, 228, 229
Ejagham (Ekoi)	223
Fang	242, 243
Western Grasslands	225-227
CHAD	
Wurkum	220-222
DEMOCRATIC REPUBLIC OF CONGO	
Boa	244
Budja	251
Chokwe	253-256
Hemba	245
Kuba	263-265
Lwalwa	252
Pende	257-260
Songye	246-250
Woyo	266
Yombe	261, 262

Country and People	Figure Numbers
EQUATORIAL GUINEA	
Fang	242, 243
GABON	
Fang	242, 243
Kwele	239-241
Punu	230-238
GHANA	
Ligbi	29
Nfana	28
GUINEA	
Baga	5-8
Koranko	10
Toma (Loma)	9
GUINEA BISSAU (BISSAGOS ISLANDS)	
Bidjogo	1-4
IVORY COAST	
Baule	24, 25
Bete	21
Dan	12-19
Kru (Grebo)	22, 23
Ligbi	29
Nfana	28
Ngere (We)	20
Senufo	26, 27, 128, 129
LIBERIA	
Bassa	56, 64
Bete	21
Dan	12-19

Country and People	Figure Numbers
Gola	11
Kru (Grebo)	22, 23
Ngere (We)	20
MALI	
Bamana	123-126
Dogon	121, 122
Marka	127
Senufo	128
NIGERIA	
Afikpo	177
Anago Yoruba	190-193
Anang (Ibibio)	194-216
Ejagham (Ekoi)	223
Igbo (Ibo)	163-170
Ijo	172-175
Ijo (?)	176
Izzi	171
Ogoni	145-158, 162
Ogoni (?)	159-161
Katana (Mama)	217
Mumuye	218, 219
Wurkum	220-222
Yoruba	178-189
SIERRA LEONE	
Limba	33
Mende	34-39, 41-44, 48, 50-53, 57-60
Sherbro	40, 45, 47, 49, 63
Temne	30-32, 54, 55, 61, 62, 71- 120
Temne or Lokko	65-70
Vai	46